the NANTUCKET *holiday* TABLE

FOR JACKIE,
I WISH YOU MANY HAPPY &
DELICIOUS HOLIDAYS!

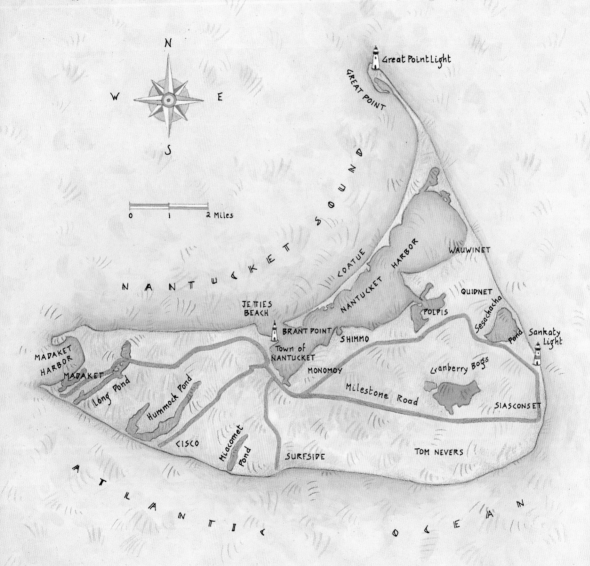

the
NANTUCKET
holiday TABLE

Susan Simon

PHOTOGRAPHS BY *Jeffrey Allen*

CHRONICLE BOOKS
SAN FRANCISCO

FOR AUNT EVELYN, WHO IS PART OF
ALL MY HOLIDAY CELEBRATIONS

Text copyright © 2000 by Susan Simon.
Photographs copyright © 2000 by Jeffrey Allen.
Map copyright © 1998 by Françoise Humbert.
All rights reserved. No part of this book may be reproduced in any
    form without written permission from the publisher.

Library of Congress Cataloging-in-Publication Data:

Simon, Susan.
    The Nantucket holiday table/ by Susan Simon; photographs by Jeffrey Allen
            p. cm.
    Includes bibliographical references and index.
    ISBN 0-8118-2508-6
    1. Holiday cookery–Massachusetts–Nantucket   2. Cookery, American–New
England style.
    TX739.S483 2000
    641.5'68'0974497–dc21   99-049719
                                             CIP

Printed in Hong Kong

Prop and food styling by Susan Simon
Designed and typeset by Anne Galperin

Distributed in Canada by Raincoast Books
8680 Cambie Street
Vancouver, British Columbia V6P 6M9

10 9 8 7 6 5 4 3 2 1

Chronicle Books LLC
85 Second Street
San Francisco, California 94105

www.chroniclebooks.com

INTRODUCTION

"WHAT'S THE ISLAND LIKE IN THE WINTERTIME?"
is the question most asked by Nantucket summertime visitors.

First of all, and lucky for the Islanders, winter arrives in Nantucket a little later than it does in mainland New England, warmed as it is by the surrounding Gulf Stream. Winter comes to Nantucket slowly, surreptitiously creeping along, so that when it finally arrives, you wonder what happened and why it's now cold and desolate.

There are positively languid September days when the Island goes very quiet, the din of wall-to-wall cars suddenly absent. The ocean water is still warm enough for a swim, and there's the exhilarating sight of leaf colors just beginning to change. Evenings are crisp and clear, and most restaurants are open, still offering imaginative selections made with the Island's own seafood and produce.

For me, October is the most glorious of all the months on Nantucket. There's a soupçon of the approaching winter in the air, just enough to stimulate and heighten the senses. The sun starts to get a bit lower in the sky. The sky's reflection on the water—or is it the other way around—helps to create the purest, most startling colors on the land. The moors are deep, deep burgundy and ochre scrub with patches of celadon and olive grasses; the sky, cabochon sapphire. On Columbus Day weekend, the Island fills up again—just briefly.

On the first day of November, the commercial scalloping season opens, and Nantucket almost looks like the working seaport it once was, with scallop boats occupying the berths in the marina that just a few months before were home port to million-dollar yachts. The austere look of winter is only hinted at as the trees begin to lose their leaves. However, the sun still warms the earth, and the bleakness a few weeks away is unimaginable. In the 1950s, a new Thanksgiving tradition was inaugurated when summer residents began to come back to the Island for one last visit, marked by a grand holiday feast, before closing their homes for the season. And so, the Island fills again with familiar and happy-to-be-back-for-an-encore faces. In December, Nantucket looks like an old-fashioned

Christmas card as Islanders take special care to decorate their historic homes with traditional bowers and garlands of evergreens, holly, winterberries, fresh fruit, and velvet ribbons. Nantucket's Main, Federal, and Centre streets are lined with Christmas trees, which are in turn decorated by one of the nearby businesses or a public school class. The town provides lights for the trees, and on the first Friday of the month, with crowds of people gathered on Main Street for the opening day of the weekend-long Shopper's Stroll, the trees are ceremoniously lit for the first time—and a collective breath is taken, broad grins decorate every face, and all seems right with the world.

There's a lovely burst of activity from New Year's Eve through Epiphany, or Twelfth Night, as Islanders continue to squeeze a few more celebrations out of the season before the *real* winter arrives with its endless gray days, when all anyone wants to do is to hibernate with a stack of good books—or to get on the first plane leaving for a hot little island.

I have very fond memories of one of my first Nantucket Thanksgivings. It was one of those unusually warm November days when, though the Island is starting to look stripped down for winter, the air is so warm you want to say, "Let's go to the beach." Which is exactly what my brother-in-law, Jimmy, and I did when we took a trip out to Sesachacha Pond on the eastern end of the Island to gather some oysters for our turkey dressing—

my sister, Laura, stayed home and made the corn bread. Those many years ago, it was easy to find oysters in the pond, which, at the time, was regularly opened to let the nearby salty ocean water in to mix with the fresh pond water, making the brackish water in which the oysters thrive. Unfortunately, these days, the pond is closed to the ocean, and its water has become completely fresh again, causing the demise of the oysters.

With cheeks flushed with the sun and lips salty with oyster brine (we sampled a few, on site, to make sure they were fit for human consumption), we returned home with our booty. Believe me when I tell you that that particular Thanksgiving dinner was one of the most delicious and satisfying meals I've ever had. From that day, I've claimed Thanksgiving as my favorite holiday, although I've never quite been able to re-create the meal we ate that day.

I've celebrated Chanukah from time to time in my life, but regret that I never have on Nantucket. In the years that I lived on the Island year round, there was a very small, almost closeted Jewish population. Now that there's a real and prospering congregation—Shirat Hayam, Song of the Sea—on the Island, it seems that during the holiday, I'm still on that other island, Manhattan, losing my mind, catering Chanukah and Christmas parties for equally frenetic New Yorkers. Someday, I'd love to celebrate the joyous festival of lights on this island, which is such an appropriate setting for candlelight.

The Christmas Day celebration that Laura, Jimmy, and I share is a hodgepodge of many traditions, Laura's and mine, and Jimmy's. Although Laura and I are Jewish, it's hard to live in the United States and not have some sort of a party on Christmas Day; after all, it's a national holiday. Santa Claus came to our house when we were young. Later in the day we would pile into the car, wearing our new sweaters and mittens made at the North Pole, leave our house in Connecticut, and head for Grandma Dora's house in Westchester, where like every other American family we would eat nonstop, stuffing ourselves senseless. Yet, even while celebrating Christmas we never lost sight of our heritage: It was manifested in our menu for the day. Sure, there was the de rigueur turkey, but there were also potato and noodle puddings, and meat "things" (savory chopped meat, peppers, and onions rolled into flaky pastry), a recipe that Dora brought with her from her native Russia. Of course, there were lots of prepackaged "leftovers," including my favorite, nut cookies, to take with us so we wouldn't starve during our ride home.

When our mother, Hilda, was alive, our Nantucket Christmas Day festivities were hilarious events. Hilda, with her keen imagination, always had wonderful presents for all of us that usually involved solving a riddle or reciting a poem written especially for the occasion. It was the presents that she created for our dogs that brought down the house. The most memorable? A mini Christmas tree that she'd decorated with plastic-wrapped, red-ribbon-tied raw chopped-meat balls. That day there was a whole lot of howling and giggling going on. Through all of this, Jimmy, whose holiday Christmas really is, would humor and egg us on, while not fully understanding the silly bond of these celebrating Jewish women. But he would reward us (and still does) anyway, with the steaming stacks of crêpes and pitchers of freshly squeezed orange juice—his family's Christmas-morning tradition—that he contributed to the party. When the high spirits began to die down, I'd break away and take the dogs out for a walk into the totally silent Nantucket evening—and I can tell you, there *was* peace on earth.

Although the Quakers, who at one time in the Island's history counted for more than 50 percent of the population, did not believe in special-day celebrations, thinking instead that all days should be special, they did reserve a bit of extra specialness for New Year's Day. New Year's Eve and Day are still extra-special days on the Island. Nantucketers in droves attend an enormous party, filled with music, champagne, and fortune-tellers, that the Nantucket AIDS Network sponsors, charging a nominal entrance fee, in order to say thank you to the community for their year-round support. Before the event starts, revelers gather at each other's homes for bountiful dinners, recalling another Quaker custom. The Quakers loved, and still do, potluck dinners. These occasions, shared among Friends, became special celebrations without being so named. Clever. Then it's on to Twelfth Night, feted with regal dinners fit for the three kings who arrived in Bethlehem on that evening so long ago.

While all the celebrations mark historical and religious events quite disparate one from another, they have one very important thing in common: They are honored with food. Lots of food. Special food, some dishes unique and specifically associated with a certain holiday—Thanksgiving and turkey, Chanukah and latkes—some just rich, as in eggnog, and others rich, as in expensive ingredients, like scallop and lobster stew.

In the almost quiet, almost privacy of wintertime Nantucket, local kitchens are bee-hives of activity as Islanders prepare their favorite holiday dishes. The solid Island citizens, accustomed to their autonomous lives, become extremely social during the holidays. And these taciturn New Englanders become voluble. Phone lines burn up as they confer with each other about a favorite family recipe, or query a new way to prepare scallops, cranberries, parsnips.

The pages of this book will show you Nantucket in the wintertime, both in spec-tacular photographs and in a verbal picture of Island activity that takes the form of recipes for the food that graces many Nantucket holiday tables. The recipes are organized into chapters on holiday breakfasts, cocktail parties, soups, sandwiches, leftovers, and food gifts, as well as the always important categories of main courses, side dishes, and desserts.

Many of these recipes are for special-occasion dishes. How often will you make Coronation Scallops for breakfast during the year? A platter of the barely cooked plump mollusks, enrobed in a pale, coral-colored curry mango chutney sauce calls out, "Look at me, I'm special." This is also a book of wintertime food. Winter produce involves slower cooking times, and very often extra ingredients that tender and brightly flavored summer produce doesn't require. However, after you've tasted Pumpkin Lasagne, or Roasted Squash Risotto, you may find yourself waiting for the first ripe turban squash as anxiously as you do the first vine-ripened summer tomato.

In the wintertime, Nantucket Island, a world-class summer resort, sheds its fancy designer duds and is once again a New England small town—albeit one redolent with history, and eyeblinkingly beautiful—inhabited with busy people who are especially busy around the holidays, making lots of good food to share with their families and friends. Here's a peek at what we cook for our favorite winter holidays. To all of you, happy holidays!

HOLIDAY
BREAKFASTS

SALMON HASH
WITH POACHED EGGS

*Hash is one of the most comforting of foods. This one, a steaming mound
of salmon and potatoes, is a treat for the tummy. With salmon available year-round on
Nantucket, it's possible to indulge yourself at will. But I like to think that
certain dishes are "special occasion" ones. This salmon hash, with its simple
and luxurious sauce of poached eggs, is destined to coddle and soothe all those
who begin a special day with it.*

1¼ pounds salmon fillet, boned,
    skin on
1 pound unpeeled red potatoes,
    finely diced
1 onion, coarsely chopped
2 tablespoons unsalted butter
½ cup heavy cream
Juice of ½ lemon (about 2 table-
    spoons)
Salt and freshly ground white
    pepper to taste
¼ cup coarsely chopped fresh dill
6 large eggs

1   In a large, covered saucepan fitted with a steamer, steam the
salmon for 10 to 15 minutes, or until the fish is opaque throughout.
Remove from the steamer and let cool.

2   Remove any salmon skin that has stuck to the steamer basket
and add water to the pan if necessary. Steam the potatoes for 10 to
15 minutes, or until a tester easily passes through a potato.

3   In a large, heavy-bottomed skillet over medium heat, sauté the
onion and potatoes in the butter until they begin to brown. Add the
cream, stir to combine, and then stir in the lemon juice, salt, and
pepper. Cook for 3 minutes more. Set aside and keep warm.

4   Skin and flake the cooled salmon. Stir the salmon into the potato
mixture and cook for 3 minutes. Turn off the heat and stir in the
dill. Cover the skillet to retain the heat while poaching the eggs.

5   Poach the eggs in simmering water. To serve, place the warm
hash on warm dinner plates and place a poached egg atop each
serving. Serve immediately.

SERVES 6

ALMOND FRENCH TOAST WITH CARAMELIZED APPLESAUCE

*"There are a good many cherry- and peach-trees planted in their streets
and in many other places. The apple-tree does not thrive well; they have therefore
planted but a few," observed* St. John de Crevecoeur, *describing Nantucket
in his vivid exploration of life in America,* Letters from an
American Farmer *(1782). I am fortunate to be the recipient of an erratic
crop from an ancient apple tree that grows on the property where I stay in
the summertime. My rare Nantucket apples are very sour, so I devised
this way to sweeten and give them a soft edge. I now spend time seeking out
companions for the applesauce. The French toast is a yummy result.*

FOR THE APPLESAUCE

4 tablespoons unsalted butter
½ cup sugar
4 pounds tart apples such as green-
    ings or Granny Smiths, peeled,
    cored, and cut into chunks

FOR THE FRENCH TOAST

1 cup whole milk
4 large eggs
2 tablespoons Amaretto (almond-
    flavored liqueur)
4 tablespoons unsalted butter
4 tablespoons sliced almonds
Eight 1-inch-thick slices challah
    (egg bread), brioche bread, or
    dense Mediterranean bread

1   Make the applesauce: In a large, heavy-bottomed saucepan, over medium heat, melt the butter with the sugar. Stir continuously until the mixture turns medium amber, then immediately add the apples. The caramel will initially harden; lower the heat and keep stirring, and it will dissolve into the apples. Cook the apples for 15 minutes or so. Much depends on how you like your applesauce, chunky or smooth. Remove from heat and reserve.

2   Make the French toast: Whisk the milk, eggs, and Amaretto together in a large bowl.

3   In a large skillet over medium heat, melt 1 tablespoon of the butter. Add 1 tablespoon of the sliced almonds and cook for 30 seconds, while soaking 2 pieces of the bread into the egg batter. Cook the bread for 1 minute on each side, or until the sides are brown and almond-covered. Keep warm in a 200°F oven while cooking the remaining bread. Serve with warm applesauce.

NOTE I usually quadruple the applesauce recipe and then freeze it in pint or quart containers for future use.

SERVES 4

BREAKFAST *and* BRUNCH

Early-American breakfasts were hearty repasts that could include a combination of foods like eggs, ham, bacon, sausage, fish, pancakes, fruit pies, doughnuts, biscuits, cakes, and bread with jams and jellies. Today, nutritionists recommend that everyone start the day with a healthy breakfast, but unless you're going out to plow the back forty afterward, it's best to eat judiciously. Brunch is more appropriate for a buffet meal. Brunch—a word, and a meal, that combines breakfast and lunch—was not invented by a clever New York restaurateur, as you might think. Brunch, in fact, was all the rage in early-twentieth-century England.

Wintertime is a holiday for the year-round residents of Nantucket, who have the Island to themselves again, and brunch is a perfect winter-holiday meal. Friends gather on the weekends at each other's homes to share food and gossip, and the Harbor House's hotel restaurant offers an incredible, all-you-can-eat brunch buffet every Sunday during the winter months.

EGGBERG

While Steve Bender busies himself creating magic in the kitchen, his Swedish-born wife, Anna, is busy weaving dreamy carpets, shawls, and Nantucket "mink" coats in her studio-shop, The Weaving Room. When I visit the Benders, I gravitate to Anna's collection of Swedish cookbooks. While I can't understand the language, I do understand the photos, and Anna obliges me with translations of things that I find interesting, like this unusual dish that looks like its namesake—an iceberg. Serve with crisp bacon and buttery toast.

8 eggs
8 teaspoons heavy cream
Salt and freshly ground pepper
    to taste

1   Preheat an oven to 325°F. Separate the eggs, pouring the egg whites in a large bowl and reserving the yolks in the shells. Add 1 teaspoon of heavy cream to each yolk. Beat the whites with an electric beater until stiff, glossy peaks form.

2   Generously butter a 9-inch quiche or gratin dish. Turn the beaten whites into the dish. Bake for 3 minutes. Remove from the oven and pour the yolks from the shells, distributing evenly in the egg whites. Return to the oven and bake for 10 minutes, or until the yolks are firmly set and the peaks of the whites are lightly browned. Sprinkle with salt and pepper and serve immediately.

SERVES 4

KEDGEREE WITH NANTUCKET SMOKED BLUEFISH

*Kedgeree is a dish straight out of the Raj, an East Indian preparation
that the British have made their own with the addition of smoked, North
Atlantic fish. Highly flavored Nantucket smoked bluefish is the perfect
fish for kedgeree. I call my version a salad because it's served at
room temperature, unlike traditional kedgeree, which has a rich
cream sauce and is served hot. ¶Serve this as part of a breakfast buffet.*

2 cups converted rice, cooked,
    drained, and cooled

2 tablespoons corn oil

2 onions, thinly sliced

1 tablespoon good-quality curry
    powder

5 hard-cooked eggs

³/₄ pound smoked bluefish, flaked

¹/₂ rounded cup Major Grey's
    chutney (mango), coarsely
    chopped

¹/₂ cup coarsely chopped fresh
    flat-leaf parsley

¹/₂ cup good-quality mayonnaise

2 teaspoons salt

1   Put the cooked rice in a large bowl. In a small skillet over
medium heat, heat the corn oil and sauté the onions until they turn
golden. Reduce heat and add the curry powder. Stir to combine and
simmer for 2 or 3 minutes. Add to the bowl of rice.

2   Cut the eggs into eighths. Reserve 8 pieces for the garnish. Add
the rest to the rice. Add the bluefish, chutney, all but 1 tablespoon
of the parsley, the mayonnaise, and salt. Gently toss with a rubber
spatula.

3   To serve, turn the kedgeree out onto a serving platter and form a
mound. Surround with the reserved hard-cooked eggs and sprinkle
the reserved parsley on top.

SERVES 8

SWEET POTATO AND CHORIZO FRITTATA SQUARES

I like any excuse to use this sausage, locally called chorice *by the Portuguese population of Massachusetts and featured in any number of dishes. Full of spices and smoked pork, it's a great accent to other foods—in this case, sweet potatoes. These delicious frittata squares fit right into any holiday brunch buffet (the addition of a thin crust makes them more portable), or you can cut them into smaller pieces for a cocktail party spread.*

FOR THE CRUST

1 cup flour

4 tablespoons cold unsalted butter, cut into small pieces

1 egg yolk

1 tablespoon ice water

1 teaspoon salt

1 teaspoon freshly ground black pepper

FOR THE FILLING

1 pound chorizo, or any spicy, smoked sausage, cut into 1-inch pieces

$^1/_2$ cup shallots, coarsely chopped

6 eggs

1 cup whole milk

Salt and freshly ground pepper to taste

$1^1/_4$ pounds sweet potatoes, cooked, peeled, and coarsely mashed

10 to 12 fresh sage leaves

1   Make the crust: Combine the flour and butter in a bowl. Use a pastry cutter or 2 knives to cut the butter into the flour until large crumbs form. Stir in the egg yolk, ice water, salt, and pepper.

2   Turn the dough into an $11^1/_2$-by-$8^1/_4$-by-1-inch baking pan (a half jelly roll pan). Use your fingers to pat the mixture evenly into the pan. Cover with plastic wrap and refrigerate for 1 hour.

3   Make the filling: Preheat an oven to 400°F. In a medium skillet over medium-high heat, fry the sausage. As soon as a bit of the fat has been rendered, add the shallots and stir. When the shallots begin to crisp, remove the skillet from heat.

4   In a large bowl, whisk the eggs and milk together until well blended. Add a pinch of salt and pepper.

5   Remove the crust from the refrigerator and pour the custard over it, completely covering the surface. Distribute the mashed sweet potatoes all over the custard. Distribute the cooked sausage and shallots over the potatoes. Scatter the sage leaves over the sausages. Bake for 35 to 40 minutes, or until the custard is well set and the sweet potatoes are browned. Cut into 9 or more squares. Serve hot or at room temperature.

NOTE   The crust can be made ahead, patted into the baking pan, and frozen until ready for use.

MAKES TWELVE 3-INCH SQUARES

CORONATION SCALLOPS ON A BED OF PARSLEYED RICE

This royal treatment for the regal Nantucket bay scallop is my adaptation of a dish served at a reception following the coronation of Queen Elizabeth II. The original preparation used chicken as the main ingredient. Sweet bay scallops are positively majestic enrobed in this creamy, subtly spicy, pale orange sauce. Serve them for New Year's Day breakfast so that the coin-shaped scallops will ensure prosperity for the coming year.

2 cups basmati or converted rice, cooked

¼ cup packed finely chopped fresh flat-leaf parsley, plus a few whole leaves for garnish

2 teaspoons salt

¼ cup corn oil

1 onion, thinly sliced

½ cup Major Grey's chutney (mango)

2 rounded tablespoons tomato paste

1 tablespoon good-quality curry powder

1 tablespoon fresh lemon juice

2 tablespoons unsalted butter

2 rounded tablespoons flour

2 cups milk

2 pounds bay scallops

1   Put the cooked rice in a large serving bowl or casserole. Add the chopped parsley and 1 teaspoon of the salt; toss to combine. Cover with aluminum foil and keep warm in a 200°F oven.

2   In a medium, heavy-bottomed skillet over low heat, heat the corn oil and cook the onion until it has wilted. Stir in the chutney, tomato paste, curry powder, and lemon juice. Cook for about 7 minutes, stirring occasionally. Remove from heat and let cool.

3   Purée the chutney mixture in a food processor until smooth and relatively lump-free. Reserve. (This can be made ahead and stored in the refrigerator.)

4   In a large nonreactive saucepan over medium heat, melt the butter and stir in the flour. Cook, stirring continuously with a wooden spoon, for 3 minutes. Add the milk and the remaining 1 teaspoon salt. Stir continuously until the mixture is slightly thicker than buttermilk. Add the chutney purée to the white sauce and stir to combine. Add the scallops and cook for 4 or 5 minutes, or until opaque. Pour the scallops over the parsleyed rice, scatter some parsley leaves on top, and serve immediately.

SERVES 8

SCALLOPING TREASURES

In addition to the income that awaits the hard-working scalloper at the end of a strenuous day of fishing in Nantucket's harbor for the world-famous mollusks, there is the expectation of other treasures that might come up in the dredges.

In the eighteen years that my brother-in-law, Jimmy Gross, scalloped, his dredges brought up countless interesting objects that would eventually be given as Christmas presents to my sister, and sometimes, me. These included smooth, round-bottomed ballast bottles, cobalt blue medicine bottles, ancient soda bottles, an antique car tire, a watch—still ticking (no, not a Timex). While these tangible things were exciting finds, and a great source for conversation, it was the fish other than scallops that gave Jimmy the most pleasure: The hake that surprised him by showing up on the culling board one day—hake are deep-water fish, not usually found in the harbor (the hake soon became lunch). The Sargasso Sea eel that squiggled out of the dredge netting and almost frightened his culler to death (the eel became an exceptional dinner). But most importantly, it was Jimmy's descriptions of the "scalloper's breakfast"—littleneck clams pulled up with the first tow at 6:30 A.M., icy cold and salty, opened immediately, splashed with Tabasco sauce, slurped down and chased with a shot of Southern Comfort—that made me nostalgic for the years when I was Jimmy's culler.

JIMMY GROSS'S CHRISTMAS-DAY CRÊPES

Every year, I spend Christmas Day on Nantucket with my sister, Laura,
and her husband, Jimmy. This is our tradition: We give each other lots and lots
of presents. The dogs and cats get presents, too, and both we and they get
presents from the chickens and ducks. Then Laura and I clean up,
while Jimmy treats us to the crêpes that he's been cooking since he was
eight years old. They're simple, and the batter doesn't need to rest before
cooking. Begin a new Christmas breakfast tradition in your family with
these crêpes—and one or more of the suggested fillings.

4 eggs
1 cup all-purpose flour
3 1/2 cups whole milk
Unsalted butter for frying

SUGGESTED FILLINGS

Sour cream and caviar (osetra is
   our favorite) or salmon roe
Mascarpone, thawed frozen
   raspberries, and maple syrup
Thawed frozen strawberries and
   crème fraîche
Caramelized Applesauce (page
   20) and heavy cream
Cranberries from Cranberry
   Shortcakes (page 122) or from
   Cranberry-Beach Plum
   Cheesecake (page 129) and
   mascarpone
Any marmalade (pages 142 to 145)
   and whipped cream

1   Beat the eggs in a large bowl. Alternately add the flour and the
milk, mixing continuously with a fork or a whisk (you'll run out of
flour before milk). Keep mixing until the batter is completely
smooth and relatively thin—about the consistency of buttermilk.

2   Melt 1 teaspoon butter in a 9-inch omelette pan (Jimmy uses 2
at a time). Pour a scant 1/4 cup batter into the center of the pan and
tip it from side to side to let the batter cover the bottom, not the
sides, in a thin layer. Cook for 1 1/2 minutes, or until the edge begins
to curl and pulls away from the side of the pan. Flip the pancake
with a metal spatula and cook for 30 seconds more. Add another 1
teaspoon butter to the pan every other batch. Pile the cooked
crêpes on an ovenproof serving platter and keep warm in a 200°F
oven until all are cooked and ready to serve. Serve with a selection
of the suggested fillings.

MAKES ABOUT TWENTY-FOUR 9-INCH PANCAKES; SERVES 2 TO 6

APPLE-MOLASSES PANCAKES WITH HONEY BUTTER

*My good friend and cooking buddy Roy Finamore visited Nantucket
for the first time in the particularly glorious October of 1993. We came to the Island
for five days, and spent the entire time eating, shopping, eating, walking, and
eating. I kept a record of the feasts that we prepared for each other
and for friends. One of the more memorable meals featured these apple-molasses
pancakes. Roy made them with a few things he found around the kitchen.
I recently added the honey-butter topping because it's one more way to enjoy
the ambrosial honey that my brother-in-law, Jimmy, produces with his native
Nantucket bees. ¶Serve with crisp bacon or smoked sausages.*

FOR THE PANCAKES

3 tart apples such as Granny Smith,
    peeled, cored, and grated
1 egg, lightly beaten
4 tablespoons unsalted butter,
    melted, plus 1 tablespoon
    butter for the skillet
2 tablespoons dark molasses
1$^1/_2$ cups milk
$^1/_2$ teaspoon baking soda
1$^1/_2$ teaspoons baking powder
$^1/_4$ teaspoon salt
2 cups flour

FOR THE HONEY BUTTER

4 tablespoons unsalted butter
1 cup pure honey

1   Make the pancakes: In a large bowl, combine the apples, egg, melted butter, and molasses. Stir in the milk.

2   In another bowl, whisk together the baking soda, baking powder, salt, and flour.

3   With a whisk or dinner fork, stir the dry ingredients into the wet until just combined. Don't overdo it! There should be some lumps.

4   In a large, heavy-bottomed skillet, melt 1 tablespoon butter over medium-low heat. Swirl the butter around the pan, entirely covering it. Using a $^1/_4$-cup measuring cup, pour 3 portions of batter into the skillet. Cook for 3 or 4 minutes, or until broken bubbles appear. Use a metal spatula to turn the cakes and cook for another 1$^1/_2$ to 2 minutes, or until a crisp surface is achieved. Keep the pancakes warm on a platter in a preheated 200°F oven while repeating to cook the remaining batter.

5   Make the butter: In a small saucepan, melt the butter with the honey over very low heat. Serve the pancakes and honey butter hot.

MAKES ABOUT 16 PANCAKES; SERVES 4 TO 6

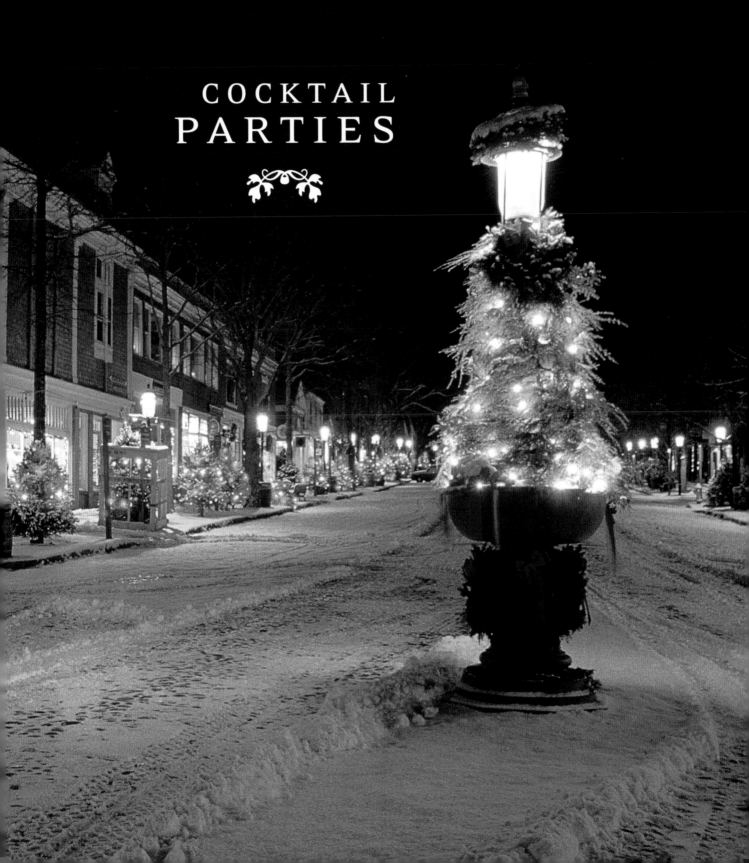

COCKTAIL
PARTIES

SCALLOP SEVICHE

It's easier than you think to make the connection between the incomparable Nantucket bay scallops and the quintessential South American preparation for raw fish, seviche. *Nantucket whaling ships that plied southern oceans often put into South American ports to process their catch and take on supplies, so it's entirely possible that more than one Nantucketer sampled some sort of raw fish marinated in citrus and onions. Citrus on Nantucket? Joseph Farnham in his memoir,* Boyhood Days in Nantucket, *published in 1914, writes, "Pickled limes brought in by ships returned from whaling voyages, were to be found in the small shops...." I like to serve seviche Ecuadoran style, with popcorn.*

2 pounds bay scallops
¹/₄ cup packed coarsely chopped
    fresh cilantro leaves, plus
    whole leaves for garnish
Grated zest and juice of I lime
    (¹/₃ cup), plus I whole lime
¹/₃ cup very finely diced red bell
    pepper
I teaspoon minced hot pepper such
    as Scotch bonnet, habanero, or
    jalapeño
4 scallions, white and green parts,
    finely chopped
I teaspoon salt
Popped popcorn

1   In a bowl, combine the scallops, chopped cilantro, lime zest and juice, bell pepper, hot pepper, scallions, and salt. Stir with a rubber spatula. Cover the bowl with plastic wrap and refrigerate for 12 to 24 hours.

2   To serve, place the chilled seviche in a pretty serving dish. Decorate with the whole cilantro leaves. Use the sharp point of a paring knife to cut the lime in half with a jagged line, then remove a tiny slice from the ends so that the halves stand up. Fill with toothpicks for spearing the individual scallops. Put the popcorn in a bowl or basket near the seviche and show your guests how to eat a scallop with a few kernels of popcorn for a new taste and textural treat.

SERVES 10 TO 12

ARCHANGELS
ON A CLOUD

The not-so-distant cousin of angels on horseback (oysters wrapped in bacon served on buttered toast), archangels on a cloud are delectable tidbits that showcase Nantucket's bay scallops. These archangels are an even more accessible cocktail party food, served on skewers and easily dipped into the horseradish cream.

1 cup sour cream

2 tablespoons heavy cream

2 tablespoons prepared horseradish, drained

1 teaspoon fresh lemon juice

$^1/_2$ teaspoon freshly ground white
   pepper

12 thin slices smoked bacon, cut in
   half crosswise

24 plump bay scallops, or 12 sea
   scallops cut in half

1   In a small bowl, combine the sour cream, heavy cream, horserad-ish, lemon juice, and pepper and stir. Refrigerate until ready to use.

2   Preheat an oven to 350°F. Place the bacon on a wire rack sitting in a baking pan. Cook for 8 minutes, or until the bacon appears to be half-cooked. Remove from the oven and increase the oven tempera-ture to 450°F.

3   Wrap a par-cooked bacon strip around each scallop and secure with bamboo skewers or wooden toothpicks. Place the loaded skew-ers on the wire rack and cook for 5 to 7 minutes, or until the scallops are opaque and the bacon crisp. Serve hot, arranged on a platter with a bowl of the horseradish cream sitting in the center.

MAKES 24 HORS D'OEUVRES

GWEN GAILLARD'S
SHRIMP TEMPURA
WITH DUCK SAUCE

*There is no Nantucket table without the food of Gwen Gaillard.
Gwen's Island restaurant, The Opera House, served up delicious food and a
sophisticated ambiance for forty fun-filled years. In addition to presiding over
the entrance to the restaurant at her proprietor's table, Gwen
entertained friends in her Nantucket and Vermont homes whenever there
was a free moment. She assures me that these shrimp were the all-time
crowd-pleasing appetizer.*

FOR THE DUCK SAUCE

One 12-ounce jar beach-plum jelly
$^1/_2$ cup finely chopped mango
    chutney
2 tablespoons finely chopped
    crystallized ginger
5 teaspoons cider vinegar
$^1/_2$ cup water
2 teaspoons sugar

FOR THE SHRIMP

2 eggs, separated
1 cup sifted all-purpose flour, plus
    some for dredging
1 tablespoon cornstarch
1 teaspoon grated fresh ginger
1 tablespoon soy sauce
$^3/_4$ cup beer, plus more as needed
24 medium-size shrimp, shelled
    (leave tail intact) and deveined
Corn oil for frying

1   Make the sauce: In a small saucepan, combine all the ingredients and bring to a boil over medium heat. Immediately reduce heat to low and simmer for 5 minutes. Let cool.

2   Make the shrimp: In a bowl, combine the egg yolks, the 1 cup flour, the cornstarch, grated ginger, soy sauce, and beer and mix to thoroughly blend. Beat the egg whites until stiff and fold into the batter. If it seems too stiff, add a little more beer. It should be like a stiff pancake batter.

3   Dredge the shrimp in flour. Place a skillet over medium heat and add enough corn oil to fill it halfway. Heat to 350°F. Dip the shrimp in the batter and fry 4 at a time for about $1^1/_2$ minutes, or until golden. Remove with a wire-mesh strainer, shake away excess oil, and drain on paper towels. Repeat until all the shrimp have been fried. Serve immediately, with the duck sauce.

MAKES 24 MEDIUM SHRIMP

ROOT-VEGETABLE CHIPS

Sweet, salty, and greasy. Heaven on earth: deep-fried chips, made with wintertime's most colorful harvest.

4 large, thick parsnips, peeled
6 large, thick carrots, peeled
4 large beets, peeled
4 cups vegetable oil
Salt for sprinkling

1   Use a mandoline or a vegetable peeler to make long, thin strips of the parsnips and carrots, and thin disks of the beets. Keep the vegetables separate.

2   In a large skillet or heavy saucepan over medium-high heat, heat the oil to 350°F. Fry the parsnips until they are golden and curled, 4 to 5 minutes. Remove from the fat with a wire-mesh strainer and shake away the excess oil. Drain on paper towels. Sprinkle with salt. Fry the carrots until they are golden and curled, 5 to 7 minutes. Drain separately and sprinkle with salt. Fry the beets until they are crisp, about 7 minutes. Drain separately and sprinkle with salt.

3   Let the vegetables cool, then toss them together to combine. Serve immediately at room temperature, or store in a container with a tight-fitting lid in a cool, dry area for up to 1 week.

SERVES 6 TO 8

MINI SWEET
POTATO AND SAGE
PANCAKES

*When winter finally arrives on Nantucket, a bit later than it does on the
mainland, the only fresh herb brave enough to tough it out in the garden is sage.
I'm always happy to use sage, not only as an accent in poultry and meat stuffing,
but also to emphasize the natural flavors of fish and vegetables.
I particularly like fried sage. The fresh leaves become unusually and pleasantly
crunchy, as in these sweet potato pancakes.*

2 pounds sweet potatoes, peeled
   and coarsely grated
1 onion, grated
3 rounded tablespoons coarsely
   chopped fresh sage
3 eggs, lightly beaten
$^1/_4$ cup flour
2 teaspoons salt
$^1/_2$ teaspoon ground cayenne
   pepper
2 tablespoons unsalted butter
2 cups corn oil

SUGGESTED TOPPINGS

Sour cream and salmon caviar
Caramelized Applesauce, page 20
Crumbled chorizo or any spicy,
   smoked sausage
Marmalade, pages 142 to 145

1   In a large bowl, combine the sweet potatoes, onion, sage, eggs, flour, salt, and cayenne. Stir with a wooden spoon to thoroughly blend.

2   In a medium skillet over medium-high heat, melt the butter with the corn oil. When the butter starts to brown, begin to cook the pancakes: Put a scant $^1/_4$ cup of the mix into the palm of your hand and flatten, forming a small 2-inch disk. Fry up to 5 pancakes at a time in the skillet. (The butter adds a nice flavor to the pancakes, but will also create foam. Five pancakes will be all that you'll be able to see at a time.) Use a butter spreader (which acts as a mini spatula) to flip the little pancakes and fry for about $1^1/_2$ minutes on each side, or until browned and crisp. Remove to a paper towel-lined baking sheet to drain. Keep warm on a serving platter in a 200°F oven until all the mixture is cooked. Serve hot with any or all of the suggested toppings.

MAKES ABOUT FIFTY 2-INCH PANCAKES

GRAVLAX WITH SPICY MUSTARD SAUCE

*While salmon are not native to Nantucket's waters, fresh salmon
is available in the local markets year round. This classic Scandinavian preparation
for curing, then serving salmon lends itself to the kind of open-house parties
that Islanders love to give around the holidays.*

FOR THE SALMON

1 tablespoon white peppercorns,
    crushed in a mortar with a
    pestle or in a food processor
$1/4$ cup kosher salt
2 tablespoons pure honey
2 tablespoons vodka
One $2^1/2$-pound center-cut salmon
    fillet, boned, skin on
Enough fresh dill to cover the fish,
    about 18 sprigs

FOR THE SAUCE

1 egg
2 tablespoons Dijon mustard
1 tablespoon English or Chinese
    dry mustard
$1/4$ cup fresh dill
1 tablespoon dill sprigs from
    marinade
1 teaspoon freshly ground white
    pepper
$1/2$ cup corn oil
$1/2$ cup crème fraîche or sour
    cream

FOR SERVING

Unsalted butter
Black bread

1   Prepare the salmon: In a small bowl, combine the crushed
peppercorns, salt, honey, and vodka and stir well. Cut the salmon in
half crosswise. Place one half skin-side down in a glass or ceramic
baking dish. Completely saturate the fish with the marinade and
cover it with dill. Place the other salmon fillet over it, skin-side up.

2   Loosely cover the baking dish with plastic wrap and weight
down the entire surface of the fish with heavy objects such as a
cast-iron skillet or cans of tomatoes. Place in a refrigerator.

3   After 12 hours, remove from the refrigerator, unwrap, and
turn the fish over. Separate the fillets and spoon the liquid that
has begun to fill the baking dish over the 2 halves. Put the fillets
together again. Re-cover with plastic wrap and weight the fish
again. Refrigerate for another 48 hours, repeating the turning and
spooning process every 12 hours. Serve now, or keep refrigerated
for up to 2 weeks.

4   Make the sauce: In a blender or food processor, combine the egg,
Dijon mustard, dry mustard, fresh dill, marinated dill, and white
pepper. Blend and process until frothy. With the motor running,
gradually add the corn oil. Use a rubber spatula to transfer the
sauce to a bowl. Fold in the crème fraîche. Cover and refrigerate for
up to 5 days.

5   To serve, place the salmon fillets on a cutting board and slice,
away from the skin, as thinly as possible on the diagonal. Serve on
barely buttered triangles of black bread with a generous dab of the
mustard sauce.

SERVES 16

SALT CODFISH FRITTERS

Wherever salt cod is available in the world, someone is making it into a ball,
a fritter, or a croquette. New Englanders are no exception. Mark Kurlansky,
author of the remarkably informative and charming Cod: A Biography of the Fish
that Changed the World *(Walker and Company, 1997), quotes*
Senator George Frisbie Hoare, a successor of Daniel Webster, who at the end
of the nineteenth century, before the entire United States Senate, praised
"the exquisite flavor of codfish, salted, made into balls, and eaten on a
Sunday morning." These little fritters, based on Puerto Rican bacalaitos,
are intended for the cocktail hour. While the popularity of salt cod
has waned a bit due to the availability of fresh cod, the tradition of bacalão
in the Portuguese kitchen and the significant Portuguese population on
Nantucket has ensured that salt cod is always for sale in the local markets.

½ pound salt codfish
2 cups flour
½ teaspoon baking powder
1 teaspoon salt
1 tablespoon minced garlic
1 teaspoon finely minced hot
    pepper such as Scotch bonnet,
    habanero, or jalapeño
¼ cup chopped fresh flat-leaf
    parsley or cilantro
2 cups water
Corn oil for deep-frying

1   Put the salt cod in a bowl and add cold water to cover. Soak for 24 hours, changing the water at least 3 times. Then put the salt cod in a saucepan and add cold water to cover. Bring to a boil, reduce heat, and simmer for 15 minutes. Remove from heat, drain, and let cool. Flake the cooled cod, removing the bones and odd bits of skin.

2   In a large bowl, combine the flour, baking powder, salt, garlic, hot pepper, parsley or cilantro, and water. Add the cod and stir with a fork to thoroughly combine.

3   In a large, heavy-bottomed skillet over medium-high heat, heat 2 inches of corn oil to 350°F. Drop the batter by teaspoonfuls into the oil, cooking 6 fritters at a time until pale gold, about 2 minutes. Remove the fritters from the oil with a wire-mesh strainer, shake away excess oil, and drain on paper towels. Keep warm in a 200°F oven until all are cooked and ready to serve. Serve hot.
The fritters may be made ahead and successfully reheated.

MAKES FIFTY TO SIXTY 1½-INCH FRITTERS

SALT CODFISH

In the early eighteenth century, the British, worried that the American colonies would try to declare independence from the Empire, began to give them some trade freedom. Besides England, the area with which trade was permitted was the British West Indies. While the Virginia colony traded tobacco and Pennsylvania traded corn, the Massachusetts colony began its salt cod-molasses trade.

Joseph Farnham (*Boyhood Days in Nantucket,* 1914) writes, "Nantucket salt-fish were everywhere especially prized. The fishermen who caught and prepared them well knew the correct knack of their preparation. Those fish were cleansed, salted and dried in a thoroughly artistic manner, and when ready for the market presented a white and attractive appearance, being especially famous because so clear and white."

And what of all the molasses that came to Nantucket? Well, the Island had a rum distillery.

CHEDDAR AND CRANBERRY CONSERVE-BUTTER TEA SANDWICHES

On December 25, 1884, Martha Fish of Cherry Grove Farm, out by Hummock Pond in Nantucket, Massachusetts, made this detailed description of the family's holiday meal in her diary: "Beautiful and clear but cool we had roast pork turnip potatoes pumpkin stewed cranberries and biscuit pudding with plums in it and sugar syrup for tea we had warm bread and butter plum cake mince and apple pie sugar cookies and cranberry tarts evening candy and apples." I imagine that these Cheddar and cranberry conserve-butter tea sandwiches would fit right in with the Fish family's menu—somewhere between "tea" and "evening."

1 cup unsalted butter at room temperature

1 cup Cranberry Conserve (page 147)

24 very thin slices whole-wheat bread

1/2 pound sharp Cheddar cheese, cut into 1/4-inch slices

1　In a bowl, blend the butter and cranberry conserve together.

2　Line up the bread in pairs. Butter each slice of bread with the cranberry conserve-butter. Cover one side of each pair with Cheddar. Top with the other side, pressing gently but firmly. Trim away the crusts. Cut each sandwich on the diagonal to make 4 triangular sandwiches.

3　Serve immediately, or refrigerate, covered with damp paper towels, until ready to serve.

MAKES 48 TWO-BITE SANDWICHES

THOM KOON'S HOT CRAB DIP

Thom Koon, Bart Cosgrove, and I began our friendship the first night of the first Shopper's Stroll in 1974. It has been a friendship marked by great shared meals and hilarious visits. Thom and Bart served this hot crab dip at the first party I attended at their Nantucket home. I loved it then, I love it now. ¶Thom thinks that he's invited to so many parties during the holidays because when he asks what can he bring, before he can finish the sentence the response is inevitably, "Oh, maybe that crab dip, if it's not too difficult." It's not, and he always brings it.

2 pounds cream cheese at room temperature

I cup whole milk

$^1/_2$ cup finely chopped onion

I tablespoon minced garlic

I tablespoon fresh lemon juice

I tablespoon prepared horseradish

Three 6-ounce cans white crab meat, drained

I teaspoon freshly ground white pepper

Salt to taste

Ritz crackers for serving

Celery sticks, carrot sticks, multi-colored bell pepper triangles, and cucumber slices for serving

1   Preheat an oven to 350°F. In a large casserole dish, combine the cream cheese, milk, onion, garlic, lemon juice, horseradish, crabmeat, and pepper. Thoroughly combine with a wooden spoon. Taste and add salt as desired.

2   Bake for 15 minutes. Stir again. Bake 10 to 15 minutes longer, or until the mixture bubbles.

3   Serve hot. You may want to keep this on a warming tray. Surround with Ritz crackers (Thom's favorite) and raw vegetables.

SERVES 15 TO 20

HOT MULLED WINE
WITH CHESTNUTS

The addition of chestnuts to any food, or beverage, in this case, is emblematic of the winter holidays. Even though native American chestnuts were all but wiped out during a blight at the turn of the century, you can find imported chestnuts everywhere around the holidays. ¶Take an afternoon walk along the beach in Quidnet, or the entire length of Sanford Farm, then come home and make this mulled wine to warm your insides and continue the glow of your hike.

1 liter full-bodied dry red wine
1 liter Madeira or sweet Marsala
18 chestnuts, roasted and peeled
Two 2-inch cinnamon sticks
1 teaspoon whole cloves
3 strips orange peel, about 2 inches
   long

1   In a large, heavy-bottomed nonreactive saucepan or stockpot, combine the wines, chestnuts, cinnamon sticks, cloves, and orange peel and simmer gently, uncovered, for 20 minutes.

2   To serve, spoon 2 or 3 chestnuts into a glass and add the hot wine. Serve with a skewer for spearing the chestnuts.

SERVES 6 TO 8

EGGNOG

In 1968, Mary Allen and Henry Mitchell Havemeyer, both descendants of early Nantucket families, the Roches and the Mitchells, opened the immensely popular Mitchell's Book Corner on the Island's Main Street. In 1976, Mary Allen co-authored, with Nancy and Arthur Hawkins, the delightful cookbook, Nantucket and Other New England Cooking *(Hastings House, 1976). The book is full of good recipes and interesting Island tidbits. The Havemeyers' daughter, Mimi Beman, who now runs the bookstore, has given me permission to use her mother's very festive eggnog recipe for this book. Mary Allen noted that "Eggnog is best when mellowed for several days before serving." ¶If you are concerned about using raw eggs, use pasteurized eggs instead.*

6 large eggs
$^1/_2$ cup sugar
$^1/_4$ teaspoon salt
2 cups heavy cream, whipped
2 cups bourbon
$^1/_2$ cup dark rum
Grated nutmeg for garnish

1   In a large bowl, beat the eggs with an electric mixer until foamy. Add the sugar and salt, continuing to beat until thickened.

2   Fold in the whipped cream. Add the bourbon and rum. Chill until ready for use.

3   Ladle from the bowl into glass cups and serve sprinkled with grated nutmeg.

SERVES 12

HOT RUM PUNCH

In the eighteenth and nineteenth centuries, many New England towns had their own rum distilleries. Quiet, Quaker Nantucket, intoxicated (no pun intended) with the new riches of whaling, had one too. While I'm not sure if early Islanders made this punch, I'd venture that certain Nantucketers that went to sea may have sampled something similar in Jamaica.

Grated zest and juice of 3 lemons
1 tablespoon grated fresh ginger
1/2 cup sugar
1 fifth Jamaican rum (dark rum)
1 cup brandy
4 cups boiling water
Orange slices studded with cloves
    for garnish

1   In a small bowl, combine the grated zest, ginger, and sugar. Use a muddler or the back of a wooden spoon to crush the ingredients together. Stir in the lemon juice.

2   In a large saucepan or stockpot over medium heat, combine the rum and brandy. Heat to the boiling point. Turn off heat. Add the lemon mixture and boiling water and stir. Cover and let stand in a warm spot for 20 minutes.

3   Pour into a preheated ceramic bowl to serve. Float the clove-studded orange slices in the bowl.

NOTE   If you have a samovar, use it to keep the punch hot. Add orange slices to a mug or glass before adding the punch.

SERVES 12 TO 16

a
NANTUCKET
GAM

A *gam* is a school of whales, but a Nantucket gam is an exchange of visits between the crews of whaling ships at sea. It's a mid-ocean party, never more welcome than during Christmastime. The poor souls out at sea for years at a time were mighty homesick thinking about their wives, children, and families at home, gathered at food-laden tables and warmed by cozy fires. Friendly faces and news were at such a premium that passing ships would brave roiling seas to come alongside each other.

According to the late Nantucket historian Edouard Stackpole, "...many ships followed an interesting custom...on Christmas day, the ship's officers would appear in the garb of apprentices and make the rounds of the mess deck, while the ship's boys would, in turn, parade the spar deck wearing uniforms and petty officer's rigs."

Another form of entertainment, observed at sea and shared with at-sea visitors thanks to the captain's largesse, was buckets of rum punch and boxes of cigars, sent from the aft quarters to the fo'c'sle. Often the captain's wife was on board for the trip, which meant that special cakes would be baked to share with the crew and their guests.

MAIN COURSES

ROASTED COD
ON A BED OF ALLIUM

In his enlightening Abram's Eyes, The Native American Legacy of Nantucket (Mill Hill Press, 1998), Nat Philbrick describes the native Nantucketers' way of cooking: "Another tradition insisted that Nantucket Indians were 'acquainted with roasting, but not with boiling.'" They made their roasting oven by digging a pit in the ground three to four feet deep, lining it with smooth stones, and then building a fire at the bottom of the pit. The stones radiated the warmth of the fire and preheated the pit for roasting. This method of cooking, taught to the settlers by the Indians, was a model for the world-famous New England clambake. Fortunately, you won't have to dig a pit in the ground in order to roast this cod. Life has become a little easier, although not nearly as adventurous.

2 pounds center-cut cod fillets
¼ cup balsamic vinegar
I cup hearty red wine
4 tablespoons pure olive oil
2 tablespoons whole fresh rose-
     mary leaves
2 teaspoons salt
2 teaspoons freshly ground white
     pepper
2 tablespoons unsalted butter
3 large onions, sliced
3 leeks, trimmed, washed well,
     halved lengthwise, and cut into
     julienne
½ cup sliced shallots

1   Place the cod in a ceramic or glass baking dish. In a bowl, whisk together the vinegar, wine, 2 tablespoons of the olive oil, the rosemary, 1 teaspoon of the salt, and 1 teaspoon of the pepper. Completely cover the cod with the mixture. Let sit for at least 30 minutes or up to 1 hour.

2   In a large skillet over medium heat, melt the butter with the remaining 2 tablespoons olive oil, salt, and pepper, and sauté the onions, leeks, and shallots until soft. Set aside and keep warm.

3   Preheat an oven to 500°F. Roast the cod for 10 minutes, or until opaque throughout.

4   Arrange the sautéed mixture on a warm serving platter. Lift the cod out of the baking dish with 2 metal spatulas and place on top of the vegetables. Pour the pan juices over the cod and serve immediately.

SERVES 6 TO 8

WINTERTIME CODFISH CAKES WITH EGG SAUCE

This recipe is my heartfelt attempt to re-create one of my favorite Nantucket lunches. Codfish cakes with egg sauce have been served at the Island's popular Downyflake restaurant since I can remember, at least four decades. The invariable accompaniments are coleslaw and baked beans. Try these codfish cakes with Wintertime Coleslaw (page 98) and Dede Avery's Maple Syrup–Baked Beans (page 92). This is an optimum holiday luncheon.

FOR THE SAUCE

- 1½ cups whole milk
- 3 egg yolks
- 2 tablespoons fresh lemon juice
- 1 teaspoon salt
- 1 teaspoon freshly ground white pepper
- 1 rounded tablespoon cornstarch
- 2 hard-cooked eggs, coarsely chopped

FOR THE CODFISH CAKES

- ½ pound potatoes, boiled, peeled, and mashed
- 1 onion, boiled for 4 minutes and coarsely chopped
- 1 pound cod fillet, steamed, boned, and flaked
- 1 egg, lightly beaten
- 2 tablespoons Dijon mustard
- 2 teaspoons Worcestershire sauce
- ¼ cup chopped fresh parsley
- 1 teaspoon salt
- ½ teaspoon freshly ground white pepper
- ¾ cup cornmeal
- 1 tablespoon unsalted butter
- 2 cups corn oil

1   Make the sauce: Scald the milk in a heavy-bottomed, non-reactive saucepan over medium heat. In a bowl, whisk the egg yolks, lemon juice, salt, pepper, and cornstarch together. Remove the scalded milk from the heat. Add the egg mixture to the milk. Whisk to combine.

2   Return the saucepan to low heat and stir continuously with a wooden spoon in all directions over the bottom of the pan. The sauce will thicken as it cooks. When it coats the back of the spoon and runs off in a thin stream, it's ready (you don't want it too thick). Add the chopped hard-cooked eggs and stir to combine. Keep the sauce warm by placing the saucepan over a bowl of hot water and cover.

3   Make the cakes: In a large bowl, combine the potatoes, onion, cod, egg, mustard, Worcestershire sauce, parsley, salt, and pepper. Wet your hands before forming each cake. Make 3-inch-diameter cakes about 1½ inches thick, pressing each carefully to assure a firm, solid patty. Thoroughly coat the cakes in the cornmeal.

4   In a medium skillet over medium-high heat, melt the butter with the corn oil. When the butter begins to brown, fry the cakes for 3 minutes on each side, or until golden. Drain on paper towels.

5   Carefully reheat the egg sauce over low heat. Spoon the warm sauce over the warm codfish cakes and serve immediately.

MAKES EIGHT 3-INCH CAKES; SERVES 4 TO 8

HOLIDAY TABLE
LOBSTER AND
SCALLOP STEW

*Lobster, shellfish, and fish have been cooked into stews since the
seventeenth century in the United States. They started out simply enough; the main
ingredient was cooked in milk, and a few fragrant spices such as mace, nutmeg,
and cinnamon were added. Then the stew was finished with butter
and served with crumbled crackers that helped to thicken the stew
and contribute texture. This lobster and scallop stew, which is a little more luxurious,
is meant for special occasions.*

1 pound cut-up lobster meat
    (cooked is okay)
1 1/2 pounds bay scallops
1/2 cup cream sherry
2 tablespoons unsalted butter
1/4 cup finely chopped shallots
1 cup finely chopped mushrooms
1 tablespoon dried tarragon
1 teaspoon sherry vinegar
2 rounded tablespoons flour
2 cups whole milk
1 tablespoon tomato paste
1 teaspoon salt
1/2 teaspoon freshly ground black
    pepper
3 egg yolks, well beaten
Toasted bread and salmon caviar
    for garnish

1   Combine the lobster, scallops, and sherry in a large bowl. Let
stand for at least 30 minutes or up to 1 hour.

2   In a large nonreactive saucepan over medium heat, melt the
butter and sauté the shallots until soft. Add the mushrooms and
tarragon and cook for about 3 minutes. Add the vinegar and then
the flour, and stir continuously for about 4 minutes to keep the
mixture from sticking. Stir in the milk and stir continuously until
the mixture begins to thicken. Add the tomato paste and salt and
pepper. Cook for 5 minutes, stirring occasionally, and remove from
heat. Add a few tablespoonfuls of the hot mixture to the egg yolks
and stir. Slowly stir the yolk mixture into the hot sauce.

3   Put the saucepan over medium-low heat and add the lobster and
scallops. Stir to combine and cook, stirring occasionally, until the
seafood is hot, about 10 minutes. Serve on warm plates with toast
and garnish with salmon caviar.

SERVES 8

COQUILLES
ST. JACQUES ALLA MODA MIA

So enamored am I of both Nantucket and Italy that there used to be a running joke between me and my sister about an imaginary flight that left from Nantucket Memorial Airport and flew directly to Poggio di Brienzone, a village in Italy's Piedmont region, where we once rented a stately farmhouse perched high on a hill. Therefore, the seemingly pretentious name of this recipe is merely sentimental.

1 tablespoon unsalted butter

1 tablespoon pure olive oil

1 clove garlic, minced

$^1/_2$ teaspoon minced hot pepper, such as Thai or cayenne

$^1/_2$ pound mushrooms, such as cremini or white button, thinly sliced

2 cups canned peeled tomatoes

$^1/_2$ cup heavy cream

1 teaspoon salt

$^3/_4$ pound whole spinach leaves, washed and stems removed

$1^1/_2$ pounds bay scallops

4 strips smoked bacon, cooked and crumbled

1 In a medium skillet over medium heat, melt the butter with the olive oil and sauté the garlic and hot pepper until the garlic starts to brown. Add the mushrooms and cook for 5 minutes, stirring occasionally. Add the tomatoes, cream, and salt and cook for 10 minutes, stirring occasionally. Combine the spinach with the other ingredients and cook for 3 minutes. Remove from heat, add the scallops, and stir to combine.

2 Preheat an oven to 450°F. Divide the scallop mixture among 6 large baking shells or individual gratin dishes. Sprinkle the crumbled bacon over the top. Bake for 8 minutes, or until the juices are bubbling around the sides of the dish and the scallops are opaque. Serve immediately.

NOTE You can make this recipe ahead of time up to adding the spinach. Reheat, add the spinach and scallops, and bake just before serving.

SERVES 6 TO 8

BAKED PLAICE WITH MUSTARD AND HERBED BREAD CRUMBS

Doing research at the library of the Nantucket Historical Association was a privilege. Staffer Libby Oldham provided me with white cotton gloves so I could read the diaries, journals, and letters written by Islanders over several centuries. Holding the fragile pages in my hands, I could imagine what William Starbuck was feeling when he wrote in his journal entry of December 25, 1886: "Christmas, fine weather. Wind westerly and light...." I noticed that plaice fish was mentioned as one of the entrees for Christmas dinner on more than one occasion. Plaice is the old-fashioned name for flounder, and every now and then the local fish shops will list plaice for sale. It's flounder. Buy it, and make this.

4 tablespoons unsalted butter

1 rounded tablespoon Dijon
    mustard

$^{1}/_{4}$ cup dry white vermouth

1$^{1}/_{2}$ pounds flounder fillets, about
    6 or 7 pieces

Salt and freshly ground white
    pepper

4 scallions, white and green parts,
    thinly julienned

$^{1}/_{4}$ cup chopped fresh dill

$^{1}/_{2}$ cup plain, unseasoned bread
    crumbs

1 In a small saucepan over medium heat, melt the butter. Add the mustard and vermouth. Stir to combine. Remove from heat.

2 Preheat an oven to 450°F. Butter a gratin dish or shallow baking dish. Cover the bottom with half the flounder fillets. Sprinkle on some salt and pepper. Cover with half the scallions and half the dill. Pour half the mustard-butter sauce over the top. Distribute half the bread crumbs over it all. Cover with the remaining flounder fillets. Repeat the layering process, ending with bread crumbs. Bake for 10 to 15 minutes, or until the top is browned and the juices are bubbling around the sides of the dish. Serve immediately.

SERVES 6

GRILLED TURKEY
WITH CORN BREAD
AND OYSTER DRESSING

In a now-famous letter to his daughter Sarah, Benjamin Franklin (son of Nantucket, through his mother) wrote, "I wish the eagle had not been chosen as the representative of our country, . . . the turkey is a much more respectable bird, and withal a true native of America." There is overwhelming evidence that turkey was the fowl served at the first Thanksgiving dinner at the Plymouth colony. It's said that the Pilgrims hunted the birds, which heavily populated the surrounding woods, with help from their dinner guests, the Native Americans. ¶Traditionally, the wild turkeys of Nantucket have been accompanied with some of the seafood from the local waters. I remember a Nantucket family Thanksgiving dinner that featured turkey stuffed with striped bass and peaches. My favorite turkey is served with corn bread and oyster dressing, a typical New England preparation. Since I cook outside year round, grilling the Thanksgiving turkey has become my tradition.

FOR THE DRESSING

4 tablespoons unsalted butter

1 cup thinly sliced shallots

2 ribs celery, peeled and finely diced

$^1/_2$ pound mushrooms, coarsely chopped

1 unpeeled tart apple such as Granny Smith, cored and finely chopped

1 pint shucked oysters, drained of liquor

$^1/_3$ cup cream sherry

1 tablespoon dried thyme leaves

$^1/_2$ teaspoon ground cayenne pepper

1 teaspoon salt

$^1/_2$ teaspoon freshly ground white pepper

6 cups 1-inch-cubed stale or toasted corn bread

1   Make the dressing: In a large skillet over medium heat, melt the butter and sauté the shallots until soft. Add the celery, mushrooms, and apple and cook for 5 minutes, stirring occasionally. Remove from heat. In a large bowl, combine the oysters, sherry, thyme, cayenne, salt, and white pepper. Add the corn bread and toss to thoroughly combine. Taste for salt and add as needed. At this point, you may refrigerate the uncooked dressing and begin to cook it when the turkey goes on the grill.

2   Preheat an oven to 300°F. Generously butter an 8-by-11-by-2-inch baking dish. Add the dressing to the prepared dish and bake for $1^1/_2$ hours, or until the top is browned and crunchy. Turn the oven off and cover the dish with aluminum foil and leave in warm oven for up to 45 minutes.

3   Prepare the turkey: Rinse and pat dry the turkey. Trim away excess fat from the cavity and tail. Use your hands to gently separate the skin from the meat over the drumsticks, thighs, and breast. Insert the sage leaves and rosemary sprigs under the skin

>>>

>>>

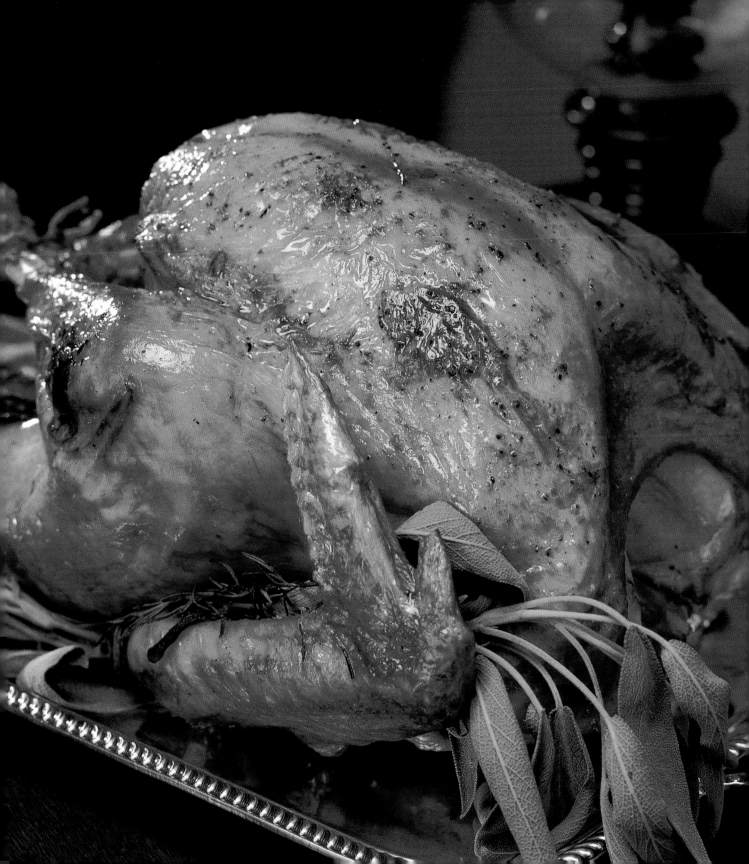

GRILLED TURKEY WITH
CORN BREAD AND OYSTER
DRESSING
continued

FOR THE TURKEY

One 13- to 14-pound turkey

12 large fresh sage leaves

Eight 3-inch sprigs fresh rosemary

Pure olive oil for coating and
    basting

Salt and freshly ground black
    pepper to taste

randomly but evenly. Pat the herbs in place. Use a pastry brush to thoroughly oil the whole turkey. Sprinkle with salt and pepper. Use butcher's twine to tie the legs together at the foot joints. Place the turkey on a rack set in a roasting pan. Fill the bottom of the pan with water.

4   Prepare a fire in a grill using one of two methods. For both methods use pieces of fruitwood that have been soaked in water for at least 30 minutes.

FOR A GAS GRILL   Divide the lava rocks in half and push them to the sides of the grill. Leave the grid off. Turn on the grill. When thoroughly heated, put a few pieces of soaked fruitwood on the rocks. Close the lid of the grill. Let smoke for 5 minutes. Place the roasting pan with the turkey in the middle of the lava rock and fruitwood "nest." Cook for $1^{1}/_{2}$ to 2 hours, basting with olive oil every 20 minutes. You may have to cover the wings with aluminum foil if they start to burn. The turkey is ready when an instant-read thermometer in the thigh reads 165°F.

FOR A CHARCOAL GRILL   Make a nest in the grill that will accommodate the roasting pan. If you are using real charcoal, there's no need for additional wood; if you're using briquettes, place the soaked fruitwood on them when they're white-hot, and replace as needed. Make sure the vents of the grill are open. The turkey may cook a bit faster in this grill. Check the temperature after $1^{1}/_{2}$ hours.

For both methods, check to make sure there's always water in the roasting pan to prevent burning. Each method should produce a burnished, bronzed-skin turkey.

5   Let the turkey rest for about 15 minutes before carving. Serve with the corn bread dressing.

Use the leftovers to make Turkey Sandwiches with Avocado and Bacon Mayonnaise (page 116), Coronation Turkey Salad in Pita Pockets (page 112), and Turkey Shepherd's Pie (page 118).

SERVES 8 TO 10

THANKSGIVING

In 1621, Governor William Bradford of the Plymouth colony declared the first Thanksgiving celebration as a way to publicly give thanks to God for an abundant harvest. In 1789, George Washington proclaimed that Thanksgiving should be an American holiday. Finally, President Franklin Roosevelt pinpointed a date, calling the last Thursday in November a legal holiday for Thanksgiving festivities.

There's no doubt in my mind that the Thanksgiving tradition made the journey to Nantucket when Thomas Macy brought the first group of settlers to the Island in 1659. The Island was blessed with a bounty of food, both on the land and from the sea, to provide the ingredients for a celebration. However, the growing Quaker population frowned on ostentatious ceremony, prefer-ring silent meditation to show their faith. In fact, many of the journal and diary entries, written one and two centuries ago, mention Thanksgiving day, but go on to describe business as usual. William Starbuck, on November 25, 1886, wrote: "Thanksgiving day, came to the office, did some writing, at 10 o'clock called on Wm. C. Dunham and tied a No. 0 truss on his right side . . . worked on trusses . . . bought some nuts and things and carried them home—ate some—read some—turned in about 11 o'clock—"

Yet, in 1889, Mr. Starbuck records, "Thanksgiving, had a turkey dinner."

Nantucket Thanksgivings still include a bit of work before settling down to a feast of shared specialties with family and friends—an early morning trip out to the harbor to scallop is not unusual on the holiday, and a good catch is one more reason to give thanks.

CHICKEN ROASTED IN A SKILLET

I love to roast chicken in a skillet. The chicken is seared over very high heat on top of the stove, then finished in the oven; the seared and roasted crispy exterior protects the interior and keeps it juicy. The technique is not unlike the reflector ovens used in many early Nantucket kitchens. Those long-ago ovens were placed at the edge of a fireplace, the front open to the flames and the back closed in order to reflect the heat. ¶This succulent chicken with its winey juices is great served with boiled and smashed little red potatoes.

$\frac{1}{4}$ cup pure olive oil

2 onions, coarsely chopped

2 cloves garlic, finely chopped

1 teaspoon finely chopped fresh hot pepper such as serrano or jalapeño

One 3-pound chicken

1$\frac{1}{2}$ cups chicken broth

1 cup hearty red wine

Juice of 1 lemon

6 carrots, peeled and cut into 1-inch pieces

3 ribs celery, peeled and cut into 1-inch pieces

3 sprigs fresh rosemary

2 teaspoons salt

1   Preheat an oven to 400°F. In a 9- to 10-inch heavy-bottomed ovenproof skillet (I use cast iron) over medium-high heat, heat the olive oil and sauté the onions, garlic, and hot pepper for 1 minute. Push the vegetables to the sides of the skillet and place the chicken, breast-side down, in the center. Sear for 4 minutes, then turn and sear on each side for 4 minutes. Finish by searing the back for 4 minutes. Add the broth, wine, lemon juice, carrots, celery, rosemary, and salt. Bring to a simmer. Place the skillet in the oven.

2   Cook for 1 hour, basting the chicken every 15 minutes.

3   To serve, remove the chicken from the skillet and carve. Place the pieces on a warm platter and cover with the pan juices and vegetables.

SERVES 4

FRIED CHICKEN FOR CHANUKAH

Every cookbook that I've read about Jewish cooking usually includes a recipe for fried chicken for Chanukah. The credit for the origin of the recipe is almost always Italy. While Italy may be the actual origin, my version celebrates the real origin: North Africa (where Chanukah was first celebrated). ¶In my interpretation, the addition of turmeric gives the chicken a golden glow like that of an oil lamp, and the spices evoke the Middle East. This fried chicken with its filigree coating will not disappoint, especially when paired with Roasted Squash Risotto (page 82) or Sweet Potato Salad with Orange Marmalade–Mustard Mayonnaise (page 96).

3 pounds boneless, skinless chicken breasts, cut into 1-by-2-inch strips

Grated zest and juice of 1 lemon

1 clove garlic, mashed through a press

1 tablespoon dried thyme

1 rounded tablespoon ground cinnamon

1 rounded tablespoon ground cumin

1 tablespoon ground turmeric

1 teaspoon red pepper flakes

3/4 cup extra-virgin olive oil

2 teaspoons salt

1 1/2 cups all-purpose flour

Corn oil for frying

4 eggs, well beaten

Lemon wedges for garnish

1   In a large bowl, combine the chicken, lemon zest and juice, garlic, thyme, cinnamon, cumin, turmeric, pepper flakes, and olive oil. Cover and refrigerate for at least 6 hours or up to 24 hours.

2   Remove the chicken from the refrigerator 1 hour before frying. Add the 2 teaspoons salt to the chicken and stir to thoroughly coat the pieces, then thoroughly coat each piece of chicken with the flour.

3   Fill a skillet half full of oil and heat over medium heat to 350°F. Dip 4 to 5 pieces of the flour-coated chicken in the beaten eggs and drop into the skillet. Cook for 1 1/2 minutes on each side, using a wooden chopstick to flip the pieces. Remove them with a wire-mesh strainer, shake away the excess oil, and drain on paper towels. Keep warm in a 200°F oven while repeating to cook the remaining pieces. Serve hot and garnish with lemon wedges.

NOTE   Don't be alarmed if toward the end of frying, the oil becomes foamy. You might clean the oil between batches with a skimmer.

SERVES 8

CHANUKAH *on* NANTUCKET

Rose and Cy Kaufman had a restaurant in Fall River, Massachusetts, before they moved to Nantucket and opened the legendary Cy's Green Coffee Pot, which catered to Islanders and visiting luminaries alike for forty-six years, from 1932 to 1978. Shirley Booth, Tennessee Williams, Thornton Wilder, Montgomery Clift, and Ogden Nash—who in 1945 wrote in Cy's guest book, "God in his wisdom made the fly and forgot to tell us why, fortunately, there are no flies on Nantucket"—all enjoyed the simple seafood and good company that was Cy's signature.

Every year during Chanukah, Cy proudly placed an electric menorah in the Green Coffee Pot's window and turned a light on every night for each of the eight nights of Chanukah. Since Cy Kaufman displayed his menorah in the restaurant's window many, many years ago, the Jewish population in Nantucket has grown enough to form a congregation. Congregation Shirat Hayam, Song of the Sea, now celebrates Chanukah as community.

DUCK BREASTS WITH CRANBERRY-ORANGE SAUCE ON WILTED CABBAGE

This is exactly the kind of dish to serve on one of the eight nights of Chanukah. Nantucket's tart, native berry is a perfect foil for rich duck meat.

FOR THE CRANBERRY-ORANGE SAUCE

2$^{1}/_{2}$ cups cranberries, picked over and rinsed

3 rounded tablespoons Sweet Navel-Orange Marmalade (page 142)

$^{1}/_{4}$ cup Grand Marnier or Cointreau

$^{1}/_{4}$ cup water

One 3-inch sprig rosemary

$^{1}/_{2}$ teaspoon freshly ground black pepper

I teaspoon salt

FOR THE DUCK

6 duck breasts

I$^{1}/_{4}$ cups hearty red wine

$^{1}/_{4}$ cup finely chopped fresh rosemary leaves

I rounded teaspoon freshly ground black pepper

I teaspoon salt

FOR THE CABBAGE

I$^{1}/_{2}$ pounds green cabbage, cored and thinly shredded

3 liquid tablespoons duck fat (see Note)

$^{1}/_{2}$ cup dry white vermouth

$^{1}/_{2}$ teaspoon salt

1   Make the sauce: In a medium nonreactive saucepan over high heat, combine the cranberries, marmalade, Grand Marnier or Cointreau, water, rosemary, pepper, and salt. Cook until the cranberries pop, about 5 minutes. Remove from heat.

2   Make the duck: Remove all but a 1$^{1}/_{2}$-by-2-inch piece of fat from the duck breasts. Reserve the fat. Score the fat on the duck in a crisscross pattern. In a large, heavy-bottomed skillet over high heat, cook the duck breast, fat-side down, for 8 to 10 minutes, or until the fat is golden and crisp. Turn over and brown in the rendered fat for 2 minutes. Add the wine, rosemary, pepper, and salt. Reduce heat to a simmer and cook until the meat is done to your taste. (Duck tastes very good rare.)

3   Meanwhile, make the cabbage: Sauté the cabbage in the duck fat, stirring to toss the cabbage so that it's thoroughly coated with the fat. Cook for 5 minutes. Add the vermouth and salt. Cook until wilted, 5 to 7 minutes more.

4   To serve, arrange the hot cabbage on a large platter. Pile the duck breasts on the cabbage and pour the pan juices over them. Spoon some cranberry-orange sauce over the duck in a decorative way. Put the remaining cranberry sauce in a bowl or sauceboat. Serve immediately.

NOTE   To render duck fat, heat trimmed and diced fat in a skillet over medium heat until it becomes liquid.

SERVES 4 TO 6

a NINETEENTH-CENTURY NANTUCKET CHRISTMAS CELEBRATION

Doctor Benjamin Sharp was Nantucket's representative to the Massachusetts State Legislature on Beacon Hill for a period at the end of the nineteenth century. Because he spent so much time "off-island," he kept up a lively correspondence with many islanders—especially women. Here's a note, dated December 29, 1898, that he received from one of his penpals, Catherine Starbuck.

... table was beautifully decorated with holly branches and flowers. At each plate was a dinner card and a bunch of pinks (your beautiful spicey flowers) from you ... 1st course oyster soup 2nd roast turkey and all the fixings 3rd ice cream-cake 4th fruit and coffee. ... After the meal was over we returned to the dining room—the gas was turned out—only light came from hall and fire. The yule log with pine boughs burned brightly. We seated ourselves in a circle and told ghost stories. ... At nine o'clock Mrs. Perry went across the hall then opened the west parlor door and called us to come. There was a room brilliantly lighted, a beautifully deco-rated Christmas tree in the centre all full of Christmas presents, baskets of candy, pictures of our celebrated Army and Navy heroes. So, we ohed and ahed and admired and munched candy awhile, then returned to the east parlor where we sang Christmas hymns.

CIDER-SOAKED BAKED HAM WITH HONEY-RUM GLAZE

In the same letter that Catherine Starbuck wrote to Ben Sharp in 1898 thanking him for the "pinks," she described a tradition of the annual Christmas dinner club: ". . . we always club together and purchase something silver or cut glass to present to the hostess. This year we bought a silver cold meat fork." Just the right serving piece for this ham. Ham is usually best served at room temperature, and this one is no exception. A cured or smoked ham like the kind used in this recipe can be found in several different cuts, all with the bone in: the butt end, the shank end, or the "picnic" shoulder. The latter is the least expensive cut, and the fattiest, but also the tastiest. It makes super leftovers, too.

One 8- to 9-pound smoked picnic
    shoulder ham
1 gallon apple cider
2 cups dark rum
Whole cloves
1/2 cup pure honey
1/2 cup packed dark brown sugar

1   Remove the rind and all but a thin layer of fat from the ham. Place the ham in a large baking dish or bowl. Cover with the apple cider and add 1 cup of the rum. Let stand at room temperature overnight.

2   Preheat an oven to 300°F. Remove the ham from the cider mixture. Reserve the cider mixture. Make diagonal cuts through the fat on the top of the ham to form a 1 1/2-inch grid. Stud a whole clove in the middle of each diamond. Place the ham on a wire rack fitted into a roasting pan. Add the marinade to the pan until it reaches the rack, but not the ham. Bake for 1 1/2 hours, basting every 20 minutes. Add more cider to the pan as needed.

3   Increase the oven temperature to 400°F. Combine the honey, brown sugar, and remaining 1 cup rum in a bowl. Whisk together to thoroughly combine. Spoon all of the glaze onto the ham, completely covering the surface and grid crevasses. Bake for 30 minutes. Remove from the oven. Let stand for at least 15 minutes or up to 45 minutes before carving and serving. Use the leftovers to make Puréed Chickpea Soup with Crunchy Ham Bits (page 108), Nantucket-Cuban Connection Sandwiches (page 114), and Chicken and Ham Croquettes (page 117).

SERVES 8, WITH LOTS OF LEFTOVERS

LOIN OF PORK WITH FENNEL SEEDS AND APPLE CREAM

Here's a roast cooked on top of the stove. While this recipe calls for a boneless loin, any pork roast will be equally successful because the milk and cream will miraculously tenderize whatever cut cooks in it.

1 tablespoon fennel seeds
2 teaspoons kosher salt
1 tablespoon minced garlic
1 teaspoon freshly ground black
   pepper
2$^1/_2$ pounds boneless loin of pork
1 cup whole milk
1 cup heavy cream
1$^1/_2$ cups diced tart apples such as
   Granny Smith
$^1/_4$ cup Calvados, applejack, or
   brandy

1   Heat a large, heavy-bottomed skillet (I use cast iron) over high heat and add the fennel seeds, salt, garlic, and pepper. Stir the mixture with a wooden spoon until the garlic begins to brown. Put the pork loin, fattiest side down, in the skillet and sear for 3 or 4 minutes. Turn and repeat until all sides are brown and covered with the seed mixture. Reduce heat to medium-low and add the milk and cream. Simmer for 45 minutes, turning every 15 minutes and spooning the sauce over the top of the roast to keep it moist. Add the diced apples. Cook for 30 minutes, continuing to turn and baste the meat. Add the liquor. Check the interior temperature of the roast; when it reaches 165°F on a meat thermometer, it's done. Or, pierce the roast with a knife—if the juice runs clear, without a trace of pink, it's done. If your roast is particularly thick, you may need to add another $^1/_2$ to 1 cup of milk to the skillet toward the end.

2   Transfer the roast to a cutting board. Cut into $^1/_4$-inch slices and arrange on a serving platter. Cover with the apple cream. Use the leftovers to make Nantucket-Cuban Connection Sandwiches (page 114).

SERVES 6

COFFEE ROAST BEEF STEW

This stew proves, once again, that necessity is the mother of invention, often with amazing results. ¶When faced with a depleted larder after a late-night arrival at her country home, a friend of mine (in the days before twenty-four-hour supermarkets) cooked her city-purchased roast beef in a pot of coffee, then declared it the best roast beef she'd ever eaten. Even though I wasn't present at that meal, I know she was right, because I've been making this stew based on my friend's story for years. ¶I like to serve this on New Year's Day with Roasted Squash Risotto (page 82).

2 pounds top round of beef, cut into 1-inch cubes
Flour for dredging
3 tablespoons unsalted butter
$^1/_2$ cup pure olive oil
4 cloves garlic, coarsely chopped
2 sprigs rosemary, about 4 inches each, or 2 tablespoons dried rosemary
$^1/_2$ cup sweet red vermouth
$1^1/_2$ cups strong coffee
Salt and freshly ground black pepper to taste

1 Dredge the beef in the flour, making sure that all sides are coated.

2 In a large, heavy-bottomed skillet over medium heat, melt the butter with the olive oil. Sauté the beef cubes a few pieces at a time until brown on all sides (adding too many pieces at once causes the ingredients to steam, not brown). Drain the beef and reserve. Sauté the garlic in the remaining butter and oil until golden. Return the beef to the skillet and add the rosemary, vermouth, and coffee.

3 Reduce heat, partially cover, and simmer for $1^1/_2$ hours, or until the meat is very tender and the sauce is thick and fragrant. About halfway through the cooking, add salt and lots of freshly ground pepper. Serve hot.

SERVES 6

FANCY YANKEE POT ROAST

Yankee pot roast, an essential New England preparation, combines two cooking techniques, braising and roasting. My Fancy Yankee Pot Roast is somewhere between a pot roast (even though I don't put it in the oven) and pot-au-feu, the French vegetable and meat soup. ¶Serve this pot roast with Pumpkin Lasagne (page 80) on the first night of Chanukah, or with Laura Simon's Root-Vegetable Latkes (page 94) for a nontraditional, cozy Christmas dinner.

1/4 cup pure olive oil

3 onions, sliced

One 3- to 4-pound top or bottom round beef roast

Flour for dredging

8 slender carrots, or fatter ones cut in half or quartered

3 ribs celery, cut in half

2 1/2 cups beef broth

1 1/2 cups hearty red wine

5 or 6 sprigs fresh thyme

I rounded teaspoon freshly ground black pepper

Salt to taste

2 tablespoons unsalted butter at room temperature

2 rounded tablespoons flour

1 In a large, heavy flameproof casserole, preferably cast iron, over medium heat, heat the olive oil and sauté the onions until golden. Thoroughly dredge the beef in the flour, covering all the surfaces. Add to the pan and brown on all sides. The flour may cause the onions to burn slightly. This is good and will add lots of flavor. Add the carrots, celery, beef broth, wine, thyme, black pepper, and salt to taste. Reduce heat, partially cover, and barely simmer for 3 to 3 1/2 hours, turning the beef occasionally. Remove the carrots and celery when they are cooked and reserve.

2 When the beef is falling-apart tender, remove it from the broth. Remove the thyme sprigs. Knead the butter and 2 tablespoons flour together until thoroughly combined. Add the mixture to the broth and stir with a wooden spoon until you have a sauce the consistency of buttermilk. Remove from the heat.

3 To serve, slice the beef and arrange on a platter. Cover with some of the sauce. Put the remaining sauce in a bowl or gravy boat. Arrange the carrots and celery attractively on the beef platter. Garnish with fresh thyme sprigs, if you like. Serve immediately.

SERVES 6

SIDE DISHES

PUMPKIN LASAGNE

There's a glorious sight on the Island toward the end of September when Bartlett's Ocean View Farm and Moors End Farm harvest their pumpkins. The orange polka-dotted fields look like huge carpets designed by Alexander Calder, and stacks and baskets of these behemoths of the squash family for sale at the farms' stands are a sure sign that a new season has arrived. ¶Make this addictive lasagne with any variety of eating pumpkin (try Sugar Pie, Sweetie Pie, or Baby Bear), or even with Hubbard or butternut squash. There are so many excellent pre-cooked lasagne noodles on the market right now that you won't be cheating if you use them.

5 tablespoons unsalted butter

1 tablespoon pure olive oil

1 onion, coarsely chopped

1 cup dry white vermouth

3 cups 2-inch-cubed pumpkin, steamed until soft

2 rounded tablespoons flour

2 cups milk

1 teaspoon freshly grated nutmeg

1 teaspoon salt

1 rounded teaspoon freshly ground white pepper

1 pound good-quality precooked lasagne noodles such as Barilla, DeCecco, or Dalverde

$^3/_4$ cup grated Parmesan cheese

10 to 12 fresh sage leaves

1   In a large, heavy-bottomed skillet, melt 1 tablespoon of the butter with the olive oil over medium-high heat. Sauté the onion until translucent. Reduce heat and add the vermouth and pumpkin. Smash the pumpkin with a potato masher or the back of a fork. Stir with a wooden spoon to combine with the other ingredients. Keep at a low simmer.

2   Meanwhile, make a white sauce: In a medium nonreactive saucepan over medium heat, melt 2 tablespoons of the butter. Add the flour and cook for 3 minutes, stirring continuously with a wooden spoon. Add the milk, nutmeg, salt, and pepper. Stir continuously until the mixture is slightly thicker than buttermilk. Add to the pumpkin mixture. Stir to thoroughly combine. Remove from heat.

3   Preheat an oven to 350°F. Use 1 tablespoon butter to butter an 11-by-7$^1/_2$-by-2-inch baking dish, then cover the bottom with sheets of precooked noodles. Spread about $^1/_2$ inch of pumpkin mixture over the noodles and sprinkle 1 tablespoon of the grated Parmesan over it. Repeat layering until all the pumpkin mixture is used, ending with a layer of noodles. Sprinkle with the remaining Parmesan. Scatter the sage leaves over the top. Dot with the remaining tablespoon of butter. Cover with aluminum foil and bake for 15 minutes. Uncover and bake for 15 minutes more, or until bubbly at the sides and golden on top. Serve immediately.

NOTE   Pumpkins are quite large and can weigh 8 pounds and more, making more than you'll need for this recipe. Freeze the leftovers in 3-cup portions for future lasagnes.

SERVES 8

ROASTED SQUASH RISOTTO

*My friend Steve Bender, who has worn many hats in his illustrious life,
from engineer to restaurateur to clammer and scalloper, has added a new
occupation to his résumé: caterer. He specializes in simple dishes that highlight
Nantucket seafood and produce. A dinner from Steve may start with
trays of just-dug (by the chef) littleneck clams and move onto this risotto
made with Steve's favorite turban squash. The squash is roasted first,
then added to the rice at the end of its cooking, so that the flavor of the squash
remains quite distinct from the rice while complementing it.*

2 pounds turban, Hubbard, or
   butternut squash, peeled,
   seeded, and cut into 1-inch
   cubes
4 tablespoons pure olive oil
1 teaspoon kosher salt
2 cups dry white wine
2 cups dry white vermouth
4 cups chicken broth
$1/2$ rounded cup coarsely chopped
   shallots (1-inch chunks)
2 cups (1 pound) Arborio, Carnaroli,
   or Vialone Nano rice
2 tablespoons unsalted butter
Salt and freshly ground pepper to
   taste
Grated Parmesan cheese for
   garnish

1   Preheat an oven to 500°F. In a large bowl, combine the squash chunks, 2 tablespoons of the olive oil, and the kosher salt and toss to evenly coat the squash. Place the chunks on a sided baking sheet or in a baking pan and roast for 15 to 20 minutes, turning occasionally so that all sides of the squash become crisp and golden. Remove from the oven and reserve.

2   In a large saucepan over medium heat, combine the wine, vermouth, and chicken broth and bring to a boil. Cook for 3 minutes, then reduce heat to a simmer.

3   In a large, heavy-bottomed skillet over medium heat on a burner near the simmering broth, heat the remaining 2 tablespoons olive oil and sauté the shallots until they begin to brown. Add the rice and stir to coat with the oil. Add 2 ladlefuls of broth mixture and stir continuously until the rice absorbs the broth. Keep adding the broth 2 ladlefuls at a time until the rice is tender and a little liquid remains in the skillet, about 18 minutes. Add the butter and roasted squash and gently fold into the risotto. Add salt and pepper. To serve, place in a warm serving bowl. Serve with grated Parmesan cheese.

SERVES 8

SQUASH

Once again, I turned to well-known Nantucket historian Nat Philbrick's information-filled *Abram's Eyes* to find out about Nantucket's early agriculture—and, of course, found the answer. Philbrick describes the Native Americans on Nantucket as "committed agriculturists, growing squash, gourds, beans.... between 400 and 1,000 years ago." To this day, summer and winter squash are grown here in great quantity and variety. Particularly versatile, winter squash is harvested in the fall and stored for winter consumption. Its thick flesh lends itself to a myriad of preparations: baked, roasted, fried, puréed, stewed, braised, and seethed. The flavor changes subtly among the varieties, from the robust turban squash to the buttery butternut to the nutty acorn squash. If you don't already, I urge you to include iron-rich, vitamin A and C laden, low-fat winter squash in your holiday larder.

STEWED SQUASH À LA NANTUCKET

In the mid-1950s, before my family began to come to Nantucket,
we spent some time exploring Cape Cod. One of my clearest memories of that time was
the painted furniture of Peter Hunt. Even as a young girl, I was struck by
his colorful and cheerful designs, which brightened an otherwise
bland decade. Peter Hunt ran his business—designer, decorator,
and world-class cook—from his home and workroom, Peasant Village in Provincetown.
Peter Hunt's Cape Cod Cookbook (Gramercy) was published in 1962,
and I'm fortunate to have a copy of this out-of-print book.
I found this recipe in it, from Eliot Cary, whose Nantucket grandmother,
great-grandmother, and great-great-grandmother cooked squash this same way.

½ cup molasses

1½ cups water

1½ pounds Hubbard squash,
    peeled, seeded, and cut into 6
    pieces

1 Combine the molasses and water in a bowl. In a large, heavy-bottomed skillet over low heat, place the squash pieces cavity-side down. Pour the molasses mixture over the squash. Bring to a boil, reduce heat, and simmer uncovered, turning the squash at least once, until it is falling-apart tender, 1 hour or longer. You may need to add more water during cooking.

Serve hot, with roasts or grilled meats.

SERVES 6

ROASTED
BRUSSELS SPROUTS
AND CHESTNUTS

*The Nantucket climate is particularly accommodating to brussels sprouts,
which need a frost to bring out their flavor, but don't want a hard freeze or
else they rot and turn to mush. Most years, the weather stays mild enough
in fall and early winter that Islanders can go into their gardens and
pick only the ripened sprouts; the others, lower on the stem, will continue
to develop.*

1¼ pounds brussels sprouts, outer
    leaves removed, bottom scored
    with an **X**
³⁄₄ pound chestnuts, scored,
    simmered for 20 minutes,
    and shelled
¼ cup pure olive oil
1 teaspoon salt
2 tablespoons fresh lemon juice
1 tablespoon unsalted butter
½ teaspoon freshly ground white
    pepper

1   Preheat an oven to 450°F. Place the brussels sprouts and chestnuts on a sided baking sheet or in a large baking dish. Add the
olive oil and salt and toss to thoroughly coat the sprouts and chestnuts. Roast for 15 minutes, using a metal spatula to turn the
sprouts and chestnuts every 5 minutes. They are finished when
both the sprouts and chestnuts look burnished and a tester easily
passes through them.

2   Place in an ovenproof serving dish and add the lemon juice,
butter, and pepper. Toss to combine and serve immediately. Or, keep
warm in a 200°F oven for up to 30 minutes.

SERVES 6

BRASSICAS

Cauliflower, broccoli, brussels sprouts, and cabbage are all brassicas, directly related to the original brassica, a wild cabbage. This seminal cabbage was native to the shores of the Mediterranean, nourished by abundant sunshine and salt-misted air—not unlike the conditions on our own Nantucket (which I've always thought of as an adjunct Mediterranean island!).

While cauliflower, broccoli, and cabbage can withstand only a light frost, brussels sprouts are reliable in the ground until Christmas. At that time, many Islanders pull up the entire plant, roots included, and put it in their cellars, then continue to pick the "little cabbages" from it as needed.

INDIVIDUAL CAULIFLOWER SOUFFLÉS

My sister, Laura, author of the elegant, information-filled Dear Mr. Jefferson:
Letters from a Nantucket Gardener *(Crown Publishers, 1998), tells me that
cauliflower varieties have some of the more suggestive names in vegetabledom,
such as Milky Way, Cashmere, Snow Crown, and Early Snow Ball.
They come in colors other than white as well, like orange and purple.
Cauliflower is rather willful and very dependent on soil temperature,
so it has a somewhat more difficult time growing on Nantucket than some of
its fellow brassicas. For a temperamental vegetable, here's a preparation that
can also be temperamental, although this soufflé is simple to make
and fun to serve.*

5 eggs, separated

1½ cups milk

¾ cup grated sharp Cheddar
cheese

2 cups steamed cauliflower florets,
coarsely chopped

½ teaspoon salt

½ teaspoon freshly ground white
pepper

½ teaspoon freshly grated nutmeg

¼ teaspoon ground cayenne
pepper

1 rounded tablespoon unseasoned
bread crumbs

1   In a large bowl, combine the egg yolks, milk, cheese, cauliflower,
salt, pepper, nutmeg, and cayenne.

2   In another large bowl, use an electric beater or a whisk to whip
the egg whites until stiff. Use a rubber spatula to carefully fold the
whites into the cauliflower mixture.

3   Preheat an oven to 325°F. Butter six 6-ounce ramekins or custard cups. Evenly distribute the cauliflower mixture among the 6
containers. Sprinkle the bread crumbs over the tops. Bake for 40
minutes, or until puffed and golden. Serve immediately.

MAKES 6 INDIVIDUAL SOUFFLÉS

BROCCOLI WITH ANCHOVY CREAM

*While many think that it was the Italians who introduced broccoli to the
United States somewhere around the turn of the century, Waverly Root, in his
book* Food *(Simon and Schuster, 1980), tells us that broccoli was being
grown in this country as early as the eighteenth century. ¶The
Italians did popularize the vegetable by showing us many ways to prepare it.
I'm partial to this method. On Nantucket, broccoli is planted twice,
producing a spring and fall crop, providing plenty of this tasty and versatile
vegetable right through the holidays.*

I¹/₂ cups heavy cream
2 tablespoons unsalted butter
I clove garlic, minced
3 anchovy fillets
¹/₂ teaspoon red pepper flakes
2¹/₂ pounds broccoli, cut into
    spears and stems peeled

1   In a small nonreactive saucepan over low heat, heat the cream
and simmer until reduced by half, 30 to 40 minutes. Add the butter,
garlic, anchovies, and red pepper flakes. Simmer for 10 minutes
more, or until the anchovies "melt" and become a part of the sauce.
Remove from heat and reserve.

2   Cook the broccoli spears in boiling water for 3 minutes. Remove
with a strainer or slotted spoon and drain on paper towels.

3   Put the drained broccoli in a large ovenproof serving bowl. Pour
the cream sauce over. Serve immediately, or keep warm in a 200°F
oven for up to 30 minutes.

SERVES 6

HARVARD BEETS WITH AN ORANGE-CAPER TWIST

Harvard beets are usually served hot because the sauce includes butter and cornstarch. However, the remarkable thing about the sauce is not its consistency so much as its sweet-and-sour flavor. Even if it's a bit of a stretch for me to call this preparation Harvard Beets, it's far too irresistible. Boston was the first place in the United States to serve these English-style beets, making this a Massachusetts recipe. I devised this variation as a way to showcase Nantucket beets.

3 pounds beets
$^1/_3$ cup cider vinegar
3 cloves garlic, finely sliced
Grated zest and juice of 1 orange,
     plus thinly julienned zest of 1
     orange for garnish
2 tablespoons pure honey
$^2/_3$ cup sour cream or plain whole-
     milk yogurt
$^1/_4$ cup coarsely chopped fresh dill
2 tablespoons capers, drained
1 teaspoon salt
1 teaspoon freshly ground black
     pepper

1   Preheat an oven to 400°F. Wrap the beets in aluminum foil, 2 or 3 to a bundle. Bake for 30 to 40 minutes, or until a tester easily passes through them. Remove from the oven. Open the bundles and let cool to the touch.

2   Peel the beets and cut them into $1^1/_2$-inch chunks. Place them in a large bowl and add the cider vinegar, garlic, grated orange zest and orange juice, and honey. Toss with a rubber spatula to thoroughly combine. Cover with plastic wrap and refrigerate for at least 8 hours; overnight is even better.

3   Remove the beets from the refrigerator 1 hour before serving. Remove the slivered garlic from the marinated beets and add the sour cream or yogurt, dill, capers, salt, and pepper. Toss with a rubber spatula to combine. To serve, turn into a serving bowl or platter and garnish with the julienned orange zest.

SERVES 6 TO 8

DEDE AVERY'S
MAPLE SYRUP-BAKED BEANS

Dede Slayton, a native of Vermont, came to Nantucket with this recipe for baked beans tucked under her arm. It wasn't long after her arrival that she met, fell in love with, and married Nantucketer Gail Avery. Was he wooed by her famous baked beans? ¶Dede and Gail disagree on the finished texture of these beans. Dede likes them crunchy, while Gail prefers them slightly mushy. I tend to side with Gail. But however they're finished, they're the best baked beans I've ever eaten.

4 cups dried Great Northern, navy, pea, or (Dede's favorite) Jacob's cattle beans
$1/4$ pound diced smoked bacon, plus 4 whole slices
1 onion, coarsely chopped
$1/2$ cup pure maple syrup
$1/4$ cup dark molasses
1 teaspoon dry mustard
1 rounded tablespoon Dijon mustard
2 rounded tablespoons catsup
1 teaspoon freshly ground black pepper
1 teaspoon salt

1   Rinse and pick over the beans. Soak them in 4 quarts of water overnight.

2   The next day, rinse the beans again and pick through them, discarding any broken or dark ones. Put the beans in a large stock-pot and add 4 quarts of water. Bring to a boil, reduce heat, and sim-mer until the beans are tender, about $1^1/2$ hours. Drain the beans, reserving the liquid.

3   Preheat an oven to 250°F. In a large bowl, combine the beans, diced bacon, onion, maple syrup, molasses, both mustards, catsup, pepper, and salt. Put the mixture in an 8-cup earthenware crock. Add 4 cups of the reserved bean broth. Place the strips of bacon on top of the beans. Cover the crock and place in the oven.

4   Bake for 6 hours, checking every hour to add more liquid as needed; I usually add between $3/4$ and 1 cup more in $1/4$-cup incre-ments. Stir before serving piping hot. The beans will keep for up to 2 weeks refrigerated. They freeze perfectly.

SERVES 10 TO 12

LAURA SIMON'S
ROOT-VEGETABLE LATKES

*Chanukah, or the Festival of Lights, is a Jewish holiday that commemorates
a victory of the Hebrews, in Jerusalem, over their persecutors, the invading
Syrians, more than two thousand years ago. As the Hebrews began to restore their
temple, which was damaged in the invasion, they found only
enough oil to fuel the lamps for one night. Miraculously, the oil burned for eight nights.
As a reminder of the miracle, part of the eight-day Chanukah celebration
includes foods that have been cooked in oil. No food is more popular than latkes.
Crisp and savory, they are the perfect accompaniment to any meat dish,
or on their own with applesauce. ¶My sister, Laura, has added parsnips
and carrots to potatoes, the traditional latke ingredient. Laura thinks that a
trip to the garden on the first day of Chanukah, pulling the roots from the cool
earth, is rather like a celebration itself.*

1¹/₂ pounds mature potatoes,
    peeled
¹/₂ pound parsnips, peeled
¹/₂ pound carrots, peeled
1 red onion, finely chopped
¹/₄ cup chopped fresh dill
3 tablespoons matzo meal or
    unseasoned bread crumbs
1 teaspoon salt
¹/₂ teaspoon freshly ground white
    pepper
2 or 3 eggs, lightly beaten (the final
    amount will depend on the
    starchiness of the potatoes)
Vegetable or corn oil for frying

1   Place a large fine-meshed sieve over a large bowl. Grate the potatoes and place in the sieve. Grate the parsnips and carrots and place in another large bowl. Add the onion, dill, matzo meal, salt, and pepper to the parsnip mixture.

2   Using your hands, squeeze the potatoes a palmful at a time over the sieve to remove as much moisture as possible. Add the squeezed potatoes to the parsnip mixture. When all the potatoes have been squeezed, remove the sieve and carefully pour off the potato liquid while leaving the white potato starch in the bottom. Add the starch to the vegetable mixture. Add 2 eggs and thoroughly combine. Put a scant ¹/₄ cup of the mixture into the palm of your hand and flatten with your other hand. If the mixture sticks together, you can form the remaining mixture into cakes. If not, add another egg and then form the cakes.

3   In a medium, heavy-bottomed skillet over medium heat, heat ¹/₂ inch vegetable oil. Place a few of the cakes in the hot oil and fry until dark gold on one side. Flip with a spatula and cook the second side until golden. Place on a baking sheet and keep warm in a 200°F oven while frying the remaining cakes. Serve hot.

MAKES ABOUT THIRTY 2-INCH PANCAKES; SERVES 6 TO 8

SWEET POTATO SALAD WITH ORANGE MARMALADE-MUSTARD MAYONNAISE

My sister, Laura, is the most determined gardener—actually, the most determined person—I know. She succeeds in growing, hands down, the most delicious sweet potatoes that I've ever tasted, and she does this in the northern climes of Nantucket Island. She claims that the soft, loamy soil on her property, combined with her warming of that soil, from planting to harvest, with black plastic mulch, coaxes her favorite sweet potato variety, Porto Rico, into a tasty tuber.

FOR THE MAYONNAISE

1 whole egg
1 egg yolk
1 tablespoon sherry vinegar
2 tablespoons English or Chinese
    dry mustard
1 teaspoon ground ginger
1 teaspoon ground cloves
1 cup bitter-orange marmalade
About 1½ cups corn oil

FOR THE SALAD

2½ pounds sweet potatoes, cut
    into 1½-inch chunks
Corn oil for coating
1 teaspoon kosher salt
2 unpeeled Granny Smith apples,
    cored and cut into ½-inch dice
¾ cup black raisins
½ cup coarsely chopped walnuts

1   Make the mayonnaise: In a food processor, combine the egg, egg yolk, vinegar, mustard powder, ginger, cloves, and marmalade and blend until thick and creamy. With the machine running, very slowly add enough corn oil to form a thick mayonnaise. Cover and refrigerate.

2   Cook the sweet potatoes in boiling water to cover for about 5 minutes. Drain and let cool.

3   Preheat an oven to 500°F. Coat the potatoes with corn oil and sprinkle with the kosher salt. Place on a baking sheet and roast until slightly browned, 20 to 25 minutes, turning every 7 minutes so that most of the sides get crunchy. Remove from the oven and let cool.

4   Put the cooled, roasted sweet potatoes in a large bowl. Add the apples, raisins, and walnuts. Add the mayonnaise and carefully, with a rubber spatula, combine with the other ingredients. Serve immediately, or refrigerate for up to 4 days (bring to room temperature before serving).

SERVES 6 TO 8

RED CABBAGE AND CRANBERRIES

When I saw this recipe in British author Delia Smith's book Winter
Collection *(BBC Books, 1996), I knew that it was destined for my Nantucket file of
things to cook. The main ingredients are locally grown, and its color is that
shade called Nantucket red made famous by the omnipresent faded
pants and caps from the Island's haberdashers. I've adapted the original recipe
here. Bright in flavor and color, this dish will bring a new dimension to
your Thanksgiving feast.*

2 tablespoons corn oil
I onion, thinly sliced
1¹/₂ pounds red cabbage, cored and
    thinly shredded
¹/₄ teaspoon ground cloves
¹/₂ teaspoon ground cinnamon
I rounded teaspoon freshly grated
    nutmeg
1¹/₂ cups cranberries, picked over
    and rinsed
I teaspoon freshly ground black
    pepper
Grated zest and juice of I lemon
I teaspoon red wine vinegar
I rounded tablespoon pure honey
I teaspoon salt

1   In a large, heavy-bottomed nonreactive skillet over medium
heat, heat the corn oil and sauté the onion until translucent. Add
the cabbage and toss with a wooden spoon to combine. Add the
cloves, cinnamon, nutmeg, cranberries, pepper, zest and juice of
lemon, vinegar, honey, and salt. Toss again to combine.

2   Cook until the cabbage wilts and the cranberries pop, about 15
minutes. Taste for salt and add as desired. Serve warm or at room
temperature.

SERVES 6 TO 8

WINTERTIME COLESLAW

Bartlett's Ocean View Farm grows the main ingredients for this coleslaw: red and green cabbage, and carrots. While their colorful produce truck ceases its Main Street stops sometime in late autumn, the farm, on the west side of the Island, stays open year round. It's worth a trip to the farm for the makings of this colorful, confetti-like salad.

1 pound red cabbage, cored and finely shredded
1 pound green cabbage, cored and finely shredded
1 pound carrots, peeled and finely shredded
1 onion, grated
1 cup good-quality commercial mayonnaise
1 clove garlic, mashed through a press
Grated zest and juice of 1 orange
2 tablespoons poppy seeds
2 tablespoons white vinegar
2 teaspoons salt
Freshly ground white pepper to taste

1   In a large bowl, combine the red and green cabbage, carrots, and onion. Toss to mix well.

2   In a small bowl, whisk together the mayonnaise, garlic, orange zest and juice, poppy seeds, vinegar, salt, and pepper. Combine the dressing with the vegetables. Chill. Bring to room temperature before serving.

This salad gets better as it marinates. It will keep up to 1 week in the refrigerator.

SERVES 10 TO 12

VIII

IX

SOUPS, SANDWICHES, AND LEFTOVERS

CHRISTMAS STOCKING
CARROT SOUP

In the December 14, 1912, holiday edition of The Inquirer and Mirror of Nantucket, Massachusetts, *there is a quarter-page advertisement from the grocer, William Holland. Among the tempting items listed for sale are "Fancy Florida oranges, sweet and juicy, 30 and 35¢ a dozen." Florida oranges continue to find their way to our winter holiday tables.*

To celebrate the orange that always filled the toe of my childhood Christmas stocking, I've created this soup made with the season's sweet carrots and finished with a swirl of orange-scented yogurt. This bright and aromatic soup is the perfect "welcome home for the holidays" meal.

2 tablespoons unsalted butter

2 tablespoons pure olive oil

1 onion, coarsely chopped

2 cloves garlic, coarsely chopped

1 tablespoon fresh thyme leaves, or 1 teaspoon dried leaves

1 rounded teaspoon ground cumin

1½ pounds carrots, peeled and cut into chunks

1 cup canned peeled plum tomatoes

6 cups light chicken broth or vegetable broth

Salt to taste

Grated zest and juice of 1 orange

1 cup plain whole-milk yogurt

A few splashes of hot pepper sauce

1   In a large, heavy-bottomed saucepan over medium heat, melt the butter with the oil and sauté the onion and garlic until the onion is translucent. Add the thyme, cumin, carrots, and tomatoes. Stir with a wooden spoon to combine. Add the broth, reduce heat, partially cover, and simmer for about 45 minutes, or until the carrots are very soft. Add salt. Remove from heat and let cool.

2   In a small bowl, whisk the orange zest and juice into the yogurt. Add a few drops of hot pepper sauce to taste.

3   In a blender, purée the cooled soup. Return to the pan. Swirl in the yogurt mixture and heat over low heat to avoid curdling the yogurt. Serve hot.

SERVES 4 TO 6

CALDO VERDE

*Caldo verde is one of the great soups of the world. I'm not kidding.
We're lucky in southeastern New England to have been introduced to this
multi-flavored and -textured soup by the Portuguese who settled here. ¶Two
ingredients are always used in this soup, kale and chorizo, called
"chorice" by the locals. Potatoes are often added. However, some cooks use beef
broth and others chicken. Some use pea beans; I like chickpeas
(another favorite ingredient in the Portuguese kitchen). ¶Double this recipe
and keep a big pot of caldo verde around to warm and nourish
family and friends.*

1/4 cup pure olive oil

1/2 cup coarsely chopped onions

1 cup thinly sliced peeled carrots

1/2 pound chopped chorizo, or other
    spicy, smoked sausage

6 cups chicken broth

1 1/2 cups thinly sliced peeled
    potatoes

1 pound kale, tough stems
    discarded, leaves rinsed and
    coarsely chopped

1 cup cooked chickpeas

1 tablespoon red wine vinegar

Salt to taste

1 In a large saucepan or stockpot over medium heat, heat the olive oil and sauté the onions, carrots, and sausage until the onions are soft.

2 Add the chicken broth and simmer for 15 minutes. Add the potatoes, kale, and chickpeas. Cook for 30 minutes more. Add the vinegar and taste for salt. Eat now, or refrigerate for up to 1 week and reheat. The longer it sits, the better it gets.

SERVES 6

CURRIED PARSNIP SOUP

"Gladiator" is the rather unlikely but apparently appropriate name for the parsnips that my sister, Laura, grows in her Nantucket garden. "They're as big as a garage, but incredibly sweet," she says. It's exactly that sweet quality of the parsnip that makes it such a good partner for a pungent curry mix. This soup is a great starter. I like to garnish it with parsnips chips made like the ones in the Root-Vegetable Chips recipe (page 38).

1/3 cup basmati rice

4 cups water

2 tablespoons unsalted butter

2 tablespoons pure olive oil

1 onion, coarsely chopped

2 cloves garlic, coarsely chopped

1 1/4 pounds parsnips, peeled and
    cut into 1-inch pieces

1 rounded tablespoon good-quality
    curry powder

6 cups chicken or vegetable broth

6 rounded tablespoons plain
    whole-milk yogurt

Parsnip chips for garnish (page
    38), optional

1   Put the basmati rice in a medium saucepan over medium-high heat and add the water. Cook the rice until it's "overcooked," 10 to 15 minutes. (The rice grains should be inflated almost to the point of splitting.) Drain and reserve.

2   In a large, heavy-bottomed saucepan or stockpot over medium heat, melt the butter with the olive oil and sauté the onion and garlic until the onion is translucent. Add the parsnips, reduce heat, and sauté for 5 minutes. Add the curry powder and stir to completely combine. Stir in the broth. Simmer for 15 to 20 minutes, or until the parsnips are soft. Remove from heat. Add the cooked rice and let cool.

3   Pour the soup into a blender 2 cups at a time and purée. Return the puréed soup to the pot. Simmer gently to reheat.

4   Serve hot, each serving garnished with 1 tablespoon yogurt and a half a handful of parsnip chips.

SERVES 6

A nineteenth-century poem

OLD-TIME THANKSGIVING DINNER AT NANTUCKET

by Lilian Clisby Bridgham

Give ear and I'll tell you a story
Of a dinner held long years ago
I'll tell it as Father's grandfather
Told him, and he surely should know.

Widow B lived alone in the outskirts
And seemed quite content with her lot.
Her garden was envied by many,
Better green goods could seldom be bought.

Each year she stored in her cellar
Apples, spuds, turnips, squashes, galore
While her shelves were weighed down with pickles
And jellies, enough for a store.

Before one Thanksgiving a neighbor
Whom some people called Deacon Slim
Knocked at the widow's back door;
Surprised, she invited him in.

"I've called, marm, with a proposition
That seems to me just can't be beat,
Folks tell me that you cook old roosters
So they're good as young chicken to eat.

"I just chopped some wood for a fellow
Who gave me a rooster for pay
A might fine idea came to me;
That's why I am here today.

"You've all kinds of vegetables, widder,
I hear you make grand mince pies, too;
And cranberry jell and plum pudding—
Folks say you're a fine cook, they do.

"Now s'posin' I chip in the rooster—
I won't charge you one single cent—
Then you ask me over for dinner
And we'll have one festive event."

"Wal, now, that sounds fair, I reckon,"
The widow replied with a smile;
"You bring the bird over real early
And I'll soon have him ready to bile."

By two o'clock dinner was ready.
He drew up his chair with a jerk,
Then ventured—"There now, don't you bother,
I'll serve it, you've done enough work."

That bird was one camouflaged creature,
Skin and bones in abundance were there;
The guest took the breast meat and runners
And the meatless wings fell to her share.

Then he piled on his plate all the fixings
'Til he just couldn't find room for more;
And he ate 'til you'd think he'd not eaten
A meal for a fortnight or more.

Now Widow B planned her cooking
To have some for Sunday to come;
But when his next plateful was eaten
And he reached for a third, she said some:

"You ate about all of the rooster,
And four-fifths of the rest of the food,
But I'll keep this little for Sunday
So your wanting it won't do you no good."

"Wal, that was a wonderful dinner,
But I've one more offer to make;
I'll take home the pies and pudding
And the bones for some soup you may take."

"Not much! Here's the frame of the creature."
Her aim was surprisingly good
And from that day he's made no proposal
His carcass to stuff with her food.

PURÉED CHICKPEA SOUP WITH CRUNCHY HAM BITS

Try this chickpea soup using your ham leftovers instead of the more usual split pea soup. The earthy, nutty flavor of the chickpeas is enriched by the ham's smoky saltiness.

8 cups water

1 ham bone, with a bit of the meat still on the bone

1 onion, cut into quarters

2 carrots, peeled and cut into 1-inch pieces

2 ribs celery, peeled and cut into 2-inch pieces

2 bay leaves

1/2 teaspoon black peppercorns

2 cups cooked chickpeas

Salt to taste

1 1/2 cups coarsely chopped ham, including some fat

1   In a stockpot over high heat, combine the water and ham bone and bring the water to a boil. Add the onion, carrots, celery, bay leaves, and peppercorns. Reduce heat and simmer for 45 minutes to 1 hour, or until the broth is full-flavored. Remove from heat and let cool. Skim the fat from the cooled broth and remove the bone.

2   Add the cooked chickpeas to the ham broth, taste for salt, and add as needed. Pour the soup into a blender 2 cups at a time and purée. Return the puréed soup to the stockpot. Simmer gently until the soup is hot.

3   Meanwhile, heat a heavy-bottomed skillet over medium-low heat. Add the chopped ham and stir with a wooden spoon to render the fat. When it seems that most of the fat has been rendered, turn up the heat and fry the ham until the bits are browned and crunchy. Lift the ham out of the skillet with a slotted spoon, add to the puréed soup, and swirl in with a wooden spoon. Serve piping hot.

SERVES 6

POTATO AND STILTON SOUP

*It's remarkable that as soon as people immigrate, settle, then prosper in a
new country, they begin to long for the trappings of the land they've fled. Early
Nantucketers were no exception, filling their homes with fine English china, silver,
and furniture with newly earned whale money. I'm wondering if a
wheel of Stilton cheese, another fine English product, might have made the trip
to our side of the Atlantic tucked into a Hepplewhite cabinet.*

2 tablespoons unsalted butter

2 tablespoons pure olive oil

1 onion, coarsely chopped

2 carrots, peeled and coarsely
    chopped

2 ribs celery, peeled and coarsely
    chopped

6 cups light chicken broth

1¼ pounds mature white potatoes,
    peeled and cut into cubes

½ cup heavy cream

¼ pound Stilton, or other hard blue
    cheese, crumbled, plus extra
    for garnish

Salt and freshly ground pepper to
    taste

3 tablespoons chopped fresh chives
    for garnish

1   In a heavy-bottomed nonreactive stockpot over medium-high heat, melt the butter with the olive oil and sauté the onion, carrots, and celery until the onion is translucent. Add the broth and potatoes. Reduce heat and simmer for 30 to 40 minutes, or until the potatoes are soft. Remove from heat and let cool.

2   Pour the soup into a blender 2 cups at a time and purée. Return the puréed soup to the stockpot. Add the cream and cheese. Simmer gently until the soup is hot, about 12 minutes. Add salt and pepper.

3   Serve in individual bowls, each topped with a scattering of crumbled cheese and ½ tablespoon chives.

SERVES 6

CHICKEN CHOWDER

This is what Harriet Pinkham, residing on Nantucket, wrote to her brother Seth on December 31, 1850: "Celebrated the last day of the first half of the 19th century by attending a chicken chowder party at Mrs. E. Congdon's." ¶Here it is, chicken chowder for not only a new century, but for a new millennium as well. Happy New Year!

One 3-pound chicken
8 cups water
¼ pound smoked bacon, finely
    diced
1 cup ¼-inch-diced peeled carrots
1½ cups ¼-inch-diced peeled
    turnips
2 cups ¼-inch-diced peeled Yukon
    Gold or russet potatoes
2 leeks, white part only, washed and
    chopped
3 sprigs fresh thyme
2 teaspoons salt
½ teaspoon freshly ground white
    pepper
4 cups whole milk
Crackers, such as oyster, pilot, or
    common

1   Remove all excess fat from the chicken. In a stockpot, combine the chicken and water. Bring the water to a simmer over medium-low heat and cook for 1 hour to 1 hour and 15 minutes. Remove chicken from the broth and reserve. Reserve 2 cups broth and store the remainder in the refrigerator or freezer for another use.

2   Put the bacon in a clean stockpot over medium heat and sauté until most of the fat is rendered and the bacon bits are crisp. Remove the bits with a slotted spoon and drain on paper towels. Remove all but 3 tablespoons of the bacon fat. Add the carrots, turnips, potatoes, leeks, thyme, salt, and pepper to the pot. Stir with a wooden spoon to combine. Add the reserved 2 cups chicken broth and lower the heat. Simmer until the vegetables are soft, about 30 minutes.

3   In another saucepan, scald the milk. Add to the vegetables. Add 2 cups coarsely chopped chicken from the reserved chicken. Add the bacon bits and heat gently. Do not boil, or the milk will curdle. Serve hot, with crackers.

NOTE   The remaining chicken can be refrigerated or frozen for future use in such recipes as Coronation Turkey Salad (page 112) or Chicken and Ham Croquettes (page 117).

SERVES 6 TO 8

TURKEY SANDWICHES WITH CRANBERRY MAYONNAISE ON SWEET POTATO BISCUITS

Use leftover turkey, mashed sweet potatoes, and cranberries to make this sandwich.

FOR THE BISCUITS

2 cups all-purpose flour
3 1/2 teaspoons baking powder
1/2 teaspoon baking soda
1 teaspoon salt
10 tablespoons unsalted butter
1 cup mashed sweet potatoes
3 tablespoons buttermilk

FOR THE FILLING

1 cup good-quality commercial
   mayonnaise
1/2 cup Cranberry Conserve
   (page 147)
Sliced turkey

1   Make the biscuits: Preheat an oven to 400°F. Sift the dry ingredients into a bowl. Using a pastry cutter or 2 knives, cut in the butter until the mixture resembles cornmeal. Blend in the sweet potatoes and buttermilk and stir until the dough forms a ball.

2   On a well-floured surface, roll the dough out 1/2-inch thick. Cut the dough with a 3-inch biscuit cutter. Place the rounds on an ungreased baking sheet. Bake until the biscuits are slightly brown, about 15 minutes. Let cool.

3   Combine the mayonnaise and Cranberry Conserve in a bowl.

4   Split the biscuits with a sharp knife. Spread the cranberry mayonnaise on the bottom half. Cover with sliced turkey and put a dab of mayonnaise in the center of the turkey. Cover with the remaining biscuit half. Serve immediately.

MAKES TEN 3-INCH SANDWICHES

CORONATION TURKEY SALAD IN PITA POCKETS

I suggest that you double the chutney purée (even though you won't need it all for this recipe) used in the mayonnaise in this recipe. The purée will keep for up to six months in an airtight container in the refrigerator. You'll find many more uses for it. Try mixing it with yogurt for a zippy crudités dip, for one. Meanwhile, you'll feel absolutely noble with every bite of this sandwich.

¹/₄ cup corn oil

1 onion, thinly sliced

¹/₂ cup mango chutney

2 rounded tablespoons tomato paste

1 tablespoon good-quality curry powder

1 teaspoon salt

1 tablespoon fresh lemon juice

1 cup good-quality commercial mayonnaise

4 cups chopped leftover cooked turkey

6 pita breads

24 watercress sprigs

1   In a medium, heavy-bottomed skillet over low heat, heat the corn oil and cook the onion until soft. Add the chutney, tomato paste, curry powder, salt, and lemon juice. Cook for 7 minutes, stirring occasionally. Remove from heat and let cool.

2   Purée the chutney mixture in a food processor until smooth. In a bowl, combine 3 tablespoons of the purée with the mayonnaise. (Reserve the remaining purée in a refrigerator for later use.) Taste and adjust the seasoning. Add the turkey and fold it in with a rubber spatula to evenly coat it.

3   Open each pita at one end and stuff it three-fourths full with turkey salad. Add 4 watercress sprigs to each sandwich. Serve immediately.

MAKES 6 SANDWICHES

SANDWICHES

In the mid-eighteenth century, John Montague, the fourth Earl of Sandwich, a chronic cardplayer, asked his servant to bring him a slice of meat between two pieces of bread, so that he could eat at the gaming table and not lose a moment of his card game. Needless to say, the pleasure of this comestible was repeated and, named after its inventor, has spread to become the world's favorite and most convenient way to eat.

Nantucket's lifestyle is well suited to sandwich consumption. Whether it's the sun-and-sea worshipers who pack a picnic lunch of sandwiches or stop on their way to the beach at one of the Island's excellent sandwich shops, or the carpenters, electricians, plumbers, and gardeners who pause to grab a bite and exchange the news of the day, a sandwich is a compact, healthy, portable meal, and not just for gamblers.

THE NANTUCKET-CUBAN
CONNECTION
SANDWICH

I was curious as to why the Cuban sandwich is so popular in Nantucket and is featured at more than one Island take-out shop. My inquiries were finally answered with the explanation that a few years ago Boston Magazine *ran a "Best Cuban Sandwich in the City" contest. Several of the better versions were transported south from the Hub and across the water to the Island.*

Dijon mustard for spreading
2 slices Portuguese bread or other
    thick-sliced dense white bread
Sliced leftover ham
Sliced leftover pork roast
2 slices Muenster cheese
4 dill pickle chips
I tablespoon plus I teaspoon
    unsalted butter

1   Spread a thin film of mustard on each slice of bread. Cover one side with sliced ham, sliced pork, cheese, and pickles. Top with the other slice of bread. Press firmly to consolidate the filling.

2   In a heavy-bottomed skillet over medium heat, melt the butter. Place the sandwich in the skillet and press it down with a metal spatula for about 3 minutes. Flip it over and cook for 2 more minutes, pressing on the sandwich with the spatula. Cut in half and serve hot.

MAKES I SANDWICH

TURKEY SANDWICHES WITH AVOCADO AND BACON MAYONNAISE ON PORTUGUESE BREAD

The dense, floury Portuguese bread made daily by several Nantucket bakeries is a good choice for these sandwiches. The compact loaf keeps the rather moist ingredients from leaking.

3 avocados, peeled and pitted
Juice of 1 lime
1½ cups good-quality commercial
    mayonnaise
8 slices smoked bacon, cooked to a
    crisp, drained, and crumbled
16 slices Portuguese bread or other
    thick-sliced dense white bread,
    toasted
Sliced turkey

1   Put the avocado pulp in a bowl. Add the lime juice and mash with a fork.

2   Combine the mayonnaise and bacon in another bowl.

3   Cover 2 slices of bread with a ¼-inch layer of the bacon mayonnaise. Cover one slice of bread with sliced turkey. Spread avocado on the turkey and top with the other mayonnaise-covered bread slice. Cut the sandwich in half. Repeat until all 8 sandwiches are made. Serve immediately.

MAKES 8 SANDWICHES

CHICKEN AND HAM
CROQUETTES

Croquettes are the quintessential way to use up leftovers. In fact, many recipes for croquettes begin by calling for "leftover chicken, boiled or roasted." What distinguishes these croquettes from others is the source of the leftovers. Combining cooked chicken with ham from the Cider-Soaked Baked Ham with Honey-Rum Glaze recipe (page 72) makes a sensational croquette, but the possible combinations are endless.

1 tablespoon plus 1 teaspoon unsalted butter

1 rounded tablespoon flour

³/₄ cup whole milk

2 tablespoons grated Parmesan cheese

¹/₂ teaspoon freshly grated nutmeg

¹/₂ teaspoon salt

¹/₂ teaspoon freshly ground white pepper

2 cups leftover cooked chicken, coarsely chopped in a food processor

2 cups leftover cooked ham, coarsely chopped in a food processor

2 tablespoons chopped fresh flat-leaf parsley

1¹/₂ cups plain unseasoned bread crumbs

Corn oil for frying

1 egg, well beaten

1   In a small saucepan over medium heat, melt the 1 tablespoon butter. Add the flour and cook for 3 minutes, stirring continuously. Add the milk and cook for another 3 minutes, stirring continuously. When the mixture begins to thicken, add the Parmesan, nutmeg, salt, and pepper. Cook, stirring until the mixture is as thick as sour cream. Remove from heat and reserve.

2   Combine the chicken and ham in a large bowl. Add the white sauce and parsley. Stir to thoroughly combine.

3   Make oblong croquettes using the palms of your hands. Press gently but firmly to keep the shape. Roll the croquettes in the bread crumbs.

4   Fill a large skillet with 1 inch of corn oil and add the 1 teaspoon butter. Heat over medium-low heat until the butter has melted and begins to sizzle. Meanwhile, pass the croquettes through the egg and then the bread crumbs again. Add the croquettes to the skillet and cook, moving them around with a wooden chopstick, for a total of 6 minutes, or until nicely browned all over. Serve hot. They may be made ahead and reheated.

MAKES 8 CROQUETTES; SERVES 4 TO 8

TURKEY SHEPHERD'S PIE

You can never have enough recipes for leftover turkey. Here's one based on a very popular chicken pie that was made for sale at my New York City take-out food shop many years ago. With the addition of cilantro to the turkey, and limey sweet potatoes for the topping, this pie might be more an Andean shepherd's pie than a traditional English one.

¹/₄ cup pure olive oil
I red onion, finely diced
2 cloves garlic, minced
I teaspoon minced hot pepper, such
   as Thai, cayenne, or jalapeño
I pound assorted mushrooms, such
   as cremini, portobello, and
   shiitake, thinly sliced
¹/₂ cup finely diced red bell pepper
¹/₂ cup heavy cream
¹/₂ cup chicken broth
3 cups diced cooked turkey
I teaspoon salt, or to taste
¹/₂ cup chopped fresh cilantro
   leaves
3 pounds sweet potatoes, cooked in
   their skins
4 tablespoons butter, melted
Grated zest and juice of I lime
I teaspoon salt

1   In a large skillet over medium heat, heat the olive oil and sauté the onion, garlic, and hot pepper until the onion is translucent. Increase the heat and add the mushrooms and bell pepper. Cook until the mushrooms have absorbed the pan juices and are tender, 10 to 15 minutes. Shake the pan from time to time to prevent sticking. Reduce heat and add the cream, broth, and turkey. Stir to combine and add salt. Remove from heat, add the cilantro, and set aside.

2   Peel the cooked sweet potatoes and put the pulp in a bowl. Add the melted butter, lime zest and juice, and salt, and mash together. Beat with a wooden spoon until light and fluffy.

3   Preheat an oven to 375°F. Put the turkey mixture in a 9- or 10-inch quiche or pie pan. Completely cover the top of the turkey with the sweet potatoes, formed into attractive peaks. Bake until the potatoes are browned, 30 to 40 minutes. Serve hot.

SERVES 6

DESSERTS

CRANBERRY SHORTCAKES

This recipe celebrates native American ingredients, from the cranberries that are our country's "first berry"—the finest of which grow on Nantucket— to the cornmeal and pecans that go into the shortcakes.

FOR THE CRANBERRIES

3 cups cranberries, rinsed and
    picked over
³/₄ cup sugar
Two 1¹/₂-inch cinnamon sticks
One 2-inch piece fresh ginger,
    peeled
I cup water
I tart, firm apple, such as Granny
    Smith, cored, peeled, and diced
I firm pear, such as Bosc, cored,
    peeled, and diced

FOR THE SHORTCAKES

1¹/₃ cups all-purpose flour
¹/₂ cup yellow cornmeal
4 teaspoons baking powder
3 tablespoons sugar
¹/₂ cup cold unsalted butter, cut
    into pieces
¹/₂ cup pecans
I egg, lightly beaten
¹/₂ cup buttermilk, plus more for
    glazing
I cup heavy cream

1 In a medium nonreactive saucepan over medium heat, combine the cranberries, sugar, cinnamon sticks, ginger, and water. Cook until most of the cranberries have popped, 5 to 7 minutes. Using a slotted spoon, transfer the cranberries to a bowl. Cook the juice until it has reduced by half to make a syrup. Remove the cinnamon and ginger. Add the apple and pear and cook until they're soft but not mushy, 10 to 12 minutes. Add the cranberries and stir to combine. Remove from heat and let cool.

2 Make the shortcakes: In a food processor, combine the flour, cornmeal, baking powder, and sugar. With the machine running, add the butter, a few pieces at a time, then the pecans, the egg, and the ¹/₂ cup buttermilk. Process until all the ingredients are just combined.

3 Preheat an oven to 450°F. Place eight ¹/₃-cup portions of dough about 2 inches apart on an ungreased baking sheet. Use a pastry brush or spoon to coat the tops of the cakes with buttermilk. Bake for 10 to 15 minutes, at most. Check after 10 minutes; the tops should look slightly brown. Let cool on a wire rack.

4 Whip the cream until thickened to the consistency of sour cream.

5 To serve, split the shortcakes in half. Cover the bottom half with cranberry mixture, then a dollop of whipped cream, and top with some more cranberries. Cover with the top half of the shortcake, set slightly askew.

SERVES 8

NANTUCKET CRANBERRIES

In a letter written by Morris Tobias in London to Captain Charles Gardner in Nantucket, on July 8, 1818, requesting fifteen whole and ten half barrels of cranberries on the first ship leaving New York in the fall (after the harvest), the premium that the world has historically placed on Nantucket's native berry becomes very clear: "... in the first place they must not cost more than from one to one dollar and a half for bushel.... The berries must be selected and picked the sound from the unsound, put up before they are quite ripe and put in spring water... you will attend to it as soon as the season will permit so that they may come as early a ship as possible, as much depends on their being here before Christmas."

Imagine the feasts that these berries, from the world's largest natural cranberry bog, brightened. Roast goose with cranberry sauce, roast lamb with cranberry-apple jelly, steamed cranberry pudding—mmmmmmm.

JANET FOLGER'S
KRUMKAKER

*Janet Folger and her husband, Charles (who's related to Benjamin Franklin's
Nantucket-born mother, Abiah Folger), celebrate Epiphany at their home in a
very traditional way. Each year, their priest prints, in chalk, the letters K.B.M.
over the threshold to their home, signifying the visit of the three
wisemen, Kaspar, Balthazar, and Melchior, to the infant Jesus. And each year,
Janet cooks a special dinner that recalls her Norwegian heritage for a party
of friends. Dessert is these krumkaker, filled with whipped cream and
lingonberries, arranged on a platter to look like the star that led the wise
men to Bethlehem. My adaptation uses a zabaglione whipped
cream and cranberries. For this recipe you will need potato flour (potato starch),
found in health food shops and most supermarkets, and a 6¹/₄-inch
krumkaker iron (see Note).*

FOR THE KRUMKAKER
6 eggs, separated
2 cups sugar
1 cup unsalted butter, melted
1¹/₂ cups sifted potato flour
    (potato starch)
1¹/₂ cups sifted all-purpose flour
1 teaspoon ground cardamom
1 teaspoon Cognac or brandy

FOR THE ZABAGLIONE
WHIPPED CREAM
8 egg yolks
8 teaspoons sugar
1 cup dry Marsala
2 cups heavy cream
Cranberries from Cranberry
    Shortcakes (page 122)

1   Make the krumkaker: In a large bowl, combine the egg yolks and
sugar and whisk to thoroughly combine. Mix in the melted butter.

2   Beat the egg whites with an electric beater or a whisk until
stiff. Use a rubber spatula to fold them into the yolk mixture.
Gradually fold in the 2 flours. When thoroughly blended, add the
cardamom and Cognac or brandy.

3   Put a 6¹/₄-inch krumkaker iron base on a burner over medium-
low heat. Spray the iron's plates with vegetable-oil cooking spray.
Close the iron and place it on the base. Heat the iron on each side
for 3 minutes.

4   Open the iron and place a rounded tablespoon of the batter in
the center of the side over the heat. Close the iron (be prepared for
a mess) and cook for about 45 seconds, then turn the iron over and
cook for another 45 seconds; the krumkaker should be pale gold.

Use a metal spatula to remove the krumkaker to a clean work surface and immediately roll on the wooden dowel that comes with the iron. Place the finished cone-shaped cookies seam-side down on a baking sheet. (Janet says that the first 3 or 4 krumkaker are always duds. It's true.) Repeat until all the batter has been cooked, scraping the excess batter from the sides of the iron's base from time to time.

5   Make the zabaglione: In a medium nonreactive saucepan, combine the egg yolks and sugar. Beat them with an electric beater or a whisk until foamy and pale yellow. Place a larger saucepan over medium heat and fill two-thirds full with water. Bring to a simmer and fit the pot with the whipped eggs over the pot with the simmering water without touching the water. Add the Marsala and beat until the mixture puffs up like a cloud. Remove from heat and place the pan in an ice-filled bowl to stabilize while whipping the cream.

6   In a deep bowl, beat the cream until stiff peaks form. Fold the chilled zabaglione into the whipped cream.

7   To serve, fill each krumkaker cone three-fourths full with the cream and the rest with cranberries. Fill a few more than the number of guests, as someone is bound to want seconds.

NOTE   This recipe makes between 35 and 40 krumkaker. But because they are so time-consuming, I suggest that even if you have fewer guests, you make the whole recipe at once rather than cut it down. Carefully store any leftover unfilled krumkaker in an airtight container for up to a week. The zabaglione whipped cream will keep for up to 5 days in the refrigerator. This way you'll be able to enjoy these melt-in-your-mouth, fragrant cookies more than once during the holidays. Or, Janet says that she's successfully stored the batter, refrigerated, for up to 3 weeks.

To order a krumkaker iron, call Sweet Celebrations at 1-800-328-6722.

MAKES **35 TO 40** KRUMKAKER

CRANBERRY CRUNCH

This is exactly the kind of sweet that you want to keep on hand as a treat for visitors who drop by to offer you the greetings of the season. It's so easy to make, even with all the distractions of the holidays.

2 cups cranberries, rinsed and
    picked over
1 cup granulated sugar
$1/4$ teaspoon ground cloves
$1/8$ teaspoon salt
$1/2$ cup chopped dates
1 tablespoon water
1 cup oats
1 cup firmly packed light brown
    sugar
$1/2$ cup chopped pecans
$1/2$ cup all-purpose flour
$1/3$ cup cold unsalted butter

1   In a medium saucepan over medium heat, stir the cranberries, sugar, cloves, salt, dates, and water together. When the mixture begins to boil, reduce heat and simmer for 5 to 7 minutes, or until most of the cranberries have popped. Remove from heat and let cool.

2   In a bowl, combine the oats, brown sugar, pecans, and flour. Use a pastry cutter or 2 knives to cut the butter in to form a crumbly mixture.

3   Preheat an oven to 350°F. Butter an 8-inch square baking pan. Put half of the oatmeal mixture in the prepared pan and evenly cover the bottom using a rubber spatula. Spread the cooled cranberry mixture over the oatmeal layer. Top with remaining oatmeal mixture. Bake for 45 minutes, or until the juices are bubbling around the sides and the top is deep gold and crisp. Cool on a wire rack. Cut into 6 or 9 pieces. You may want to quarter those pieces for one-bite morsels.

SERVES 6 TO 9

CRANBERRY BEACH-PLUM
CHEESECAKE

*Sometime in June of every year, Nantucket Island is trimmed with a lacy
border of white beach-plum blossoms—and if the birds don't get there first,
sometime at the end of August or the beginning of September, the ripened, musty,
intensely flavored beach plums will be ready to harvest. Then you'll
see the Island bordered with people, baskets over their arms, gathering the
fruit to take home and make tangy-sweet beach-plum jelly. It's this jelly,
also available commercially, that gives the topping for this cheesecake
its unique dimension.*

FOR THE TOPPING

4 cups cranberries, rinsed and
    picked over
I cup beach-plum jelly or red
    currant jelly
Grated zest and juice of I orange
I¹/₂ cups sugar

FOR THE CRUST

2 cups crushed graham cracker
    crumbs
¹/₃ cup sugar
¹/₃ cup butter, melted

FOR THE FILLING

I pound cream cheese at room
    temperature
I pound whole-milk ricotta
¹/₂ cup sour cream
IO eggs
2 teaspoons pure vanilla extract

1   Make the topping: In a large saucepan over medium-high heat, combine the cranberries, beach-plum jelly, zest and juice of orange, and 1¹/₂ cups sugar. Bring to a boil and cook for 5 minutes. Remove from heat and let cool, then refrigerate until cake is served.

2   Make the crust: In a bowl, combine the cracker crumbs, sugar, and melted butter. Stir to combine. Firmly press the mixture into the bottom of a 10-inch springform pan. Set aside.

3   Make the filling: Preheat an oven to 375°F. In a large bowl, combine the cream cheese, ricotta, sour cream, eggs, and vanilla extract and stir vigorously. Pour the mixture into the pan and bake for 1 hour, or until the top is slightly brown and the edges are beginning to pull away from the side of the pan.

Refrigerate the cake for at least 12 hours before serving. To serve, release the cake from the pan. Place on a platter and cover the top with half of the cranberries. Let the juice drip down the sides. Use the remaining cranberries to top individual servings.

SERVES IO TO I2

SPIRITED GINGERBREAD
WITH GINGER ICE CREAM

In mid-nineteenth-century Nantucket, gingerbread was not only baked at home, it was also available for sale at the Chase and Cook Bakery; according to Joseph Farnham, writing in his 1914 Boyhood Days in Nantucket, *"So much depended upon for its varied products in pastry ... that scarcely a Nantucket housewife really felt that she could successfully keep house without it ... their gingerbread was as popular as their seed cakes." Later in his memoir he writes, "Ice cream at Nantucket was ever held as one of the delectable luxuries. We used to think—perhaps we were too arrogant— that the so called 'Nantucket ice cream' was a little bit better than that anywhere else obtainable." Joseph Farnham would have loved this dessert, rich in the flavors of his childhood.*

$\frac{1}{2}$ cup unsalted butter at room
    temperature

$\frac{1}{2}$ cup sugar

1 egg

$2\frac{1}{2}$ cups sifted all-purpose flour

$1\frac{1}{2}$ teaspoons baking powder

1 teaspoon salt

$\frac{1}{2}$ teaspoon ground cinnamon

1 tablespoon ground ginger

$\frac{1}{2}$ teaspoon ground cloves

1 cup dark molasses

$\frac{3}{4}$ cup hot water

$\frac{1}{4}$ cup dark rum

$\frac{1}{4}$ cup finely julienned crystallized
    ginger

Ginger Ice Cream for serving
    (recipe follows)

> > >

1   Preheat an oven to 350°F. In a large bowl, combine the butter, sugar, and egg and beat with a wooden spoon until smooth.

2   Add the flour, baking powder, salt, cinnamon, ground ginger, and cloves. Continue to beat to combine. Add the molasses, hot water, and rum and gently stir to make a smooth batter. Stir in the crystallized ginger.

3   Butter an 8-inch square baking pan. Pour the batter into the pan. Bake for 45 minutes, or until a tester inserted in the center comes out clean and the gingerbread is beginning to pull away from the sides of the pan. Let cool on a wire rack.

4   To serve, cut into 8 squares. Cut each piece into smaller slices. Arrange on dessert plates in an attractive way and top with a scoop of ginger ice cream.

SERVES 8

> > >

GINGER
ICE CREAM

2 cups heavy cream
1 cup whole milk
One 2-inch piece fresh ginger, cut
    into thin slices and crushed
³/₄ cup sugar
3 egg yolks
¹/₄ cup finely diced crystallized
    ginger

1   In a heavy-bottomed nonreactive saucepan over low heat, combine the cream, milk, and fresh ginger. Bring to a low simmer and cook for 15 to 20 minutes to thoroughly infuse the cream with the ginger. Add the sugar and stir until dissolved.

2   Whisk the egg yolks in a large bowl. Strain in about one third of the hot cream mixture and quickly whisk. Strain in the rest of the liquid. Use the back of a large spoon to press the ginger through the strainer. Return to the saucepan. Cook over medium heat, stirring constantly, until the mixture coats the back of a spoon, 5 to 7 minutes.

3   Strain the mixture into a clean bowl. Set the bowl in a larger bowl of ice water and let cool, stirring occasionally. Remove the bowl from the ice water, cover with plastic wrap, and refrigerate for at least 8 hours, preferably overnight.

4   Add the chilled cream to your ice cream maker. Follow the manufacturer's directions to freeze. Just as the ice cream begins to freeze, fold in the crystallized ginger. Finish freezing. Serve immediately, or remove from ice cream maker and store in a plastic quart container in the freezer until ready for use.

MAKES 1¹/₂ PINTS

ORCHARD BUNDLES
WITH APPLE-CARAMEL SAUCE

This dessert is based on an apple turnover that my colleague Lori Leckman used to make for my take-out shop in New York, and the addictive little pastries that my mother made, for every special occasion and holiday until her last days, on Nantucket. I searched through her collection of recipes hoping to find a record of the flaky, buttery pastry that she wrapped around a cinnamon-nut filling. After much culling, and stops at recipes to fondly remember other things that she'd cooked for us, there it was: a few words on a piece of paper ripped out of an agenda book. ¶Here it is for you, plumped with a fruit filling and fancied up with a velvety smooth sauce.

FOR THE PASTRY

3 cups sifted all-purpose flour

1 cup unsalted butter, cut into pieces

1 cup sour cream

3 egg yolks

1 package (¼ ounce) active dry yeast

½ teaspoon salt

FOR THE FILLING

1 tablespoon unsalted butter

2 firm pears, such as Bosc, peeled, cored, and diced

2 crisp, sweet apples, such as Fuji, Empire, or Winesap, peeled, cored, and diced

½ cup dried cranberries or raisins

½ cup chopped walnuts

⅓ cup packed dark brown sugar

1 teaspoon ground cinnamon

> > >

1   Make the pastry: In a bowl, combine the flour and butter. Cut the butter into the flour with a pastry cutter or 2 knives until large crumbs form. Add the sour cream, yolks, yeast, and salt. Stir to thoroughly combine. Turn out onto a clean, floured work surface and knead for 2 or 3 minutes until the dough is compact. Cut the dough into 8 equal parts. Form into disks and flatten. Wrap the disks in plastic wrap or waxed paper and refrigerate for at least 4 hours.

2   Make the filling: In a large skillet over medium heat, melt the butter and stir in the pears, apples, cranberries or raisins, walnuts, brown sugar, and cinnamon. Cook for 5 to 7 minutes, or until the fruit is tender but not mushy. Remove from heat.

3   Preheat an oven to 375°F. Line a baking sheet with parchment paper. On a lightly floured work surface, roll 1 pastry disk at a time into a thin circle. Place one-eighth of the fruit filling in the center of each disk. Gather the pastry, as you might a piece of fabric, to the center. Pull together the excess dough and twist to form a flower-shaped knob on top. Place on the prepared pan. Bake in the center of the oven until the entire surface of the bundles is deep gold, about 30 minutes. If, after 20 minutes, the top is getting too brown, cover with aluminum foil and continue to cook the full 30 minutes. Let cool on a wire rack.

> > >

ORCHARD BUNDLES WITH
APPLE-CARAMEL SAUCE
continued

FOR THE SAUCE
I crisp, sweet apple (see above),
  peeled, cored, and diced
$^1/_2$ cup granulated sugar
2 tablespoons water
I cup heavy cream

4   Make the sauce: In a small saucepan over low heat, cook the diced apple, stirring occasionally, until the apple is soft, 10 to 15 minutes. Let cool, then press through a sieve with the back of a large spoon; you should have about $^1/_4$ cup apple purée. Set aside. In a small saucepan over medium heat, combine the sugar and water and stir continuously until amber-colored. Add the cream. The caramel will immediately harden. Continue to stir and it will dissolve. Finally, add the apple purée. Stir and remove from heat.

To serve, place each orchard bundle on a dessert plate and surround with a stream of caramel sauce. Put any leftover sauce in a pitcher or a small bowl and bring to the table.

SERVES 8

THE CONTESSA'S BREAD PUDDING

My friend Contessa Nally Bellati, true to her half-English heritage, regards "pudding" (British for dessert) as her favorite part of a meal. In the more than thirty years of our friendship, Nally has made more versions of trifle and bread pudding than I can remember. What I do remember is how much I loved them all. Here's a bread pudding that she made one Thanksgiving on one of her not infrequent visits to the Island.

1 crusty baguette (not a ficelle), about 18 inches long

4 tablespoons unsalted butter at room temperature

$^1/_2$ cup Sweet Navel-Orange Marmalade (page 142)

2 crisp, sweet apples such as Gala, Fuji, or Golden Delicious, peeled, cored, and thinly sliced

$^1/_2$ cup dried cranberries or raisins

4 eggs

1 teaspoon pure vanilla extract

1 tablespoon Grand Marnier or Cointreau

$2^1/_2$ cups whole milk

$^1/_2$ cup heavy cream

$^1/_4$ cup sugar

1   Preheat an oven to 350°F. Cut the baguette into $^1/_2$-inch slices. Butter the bread and cover each slice with marmalade.

2   Butter an 8-cup baking dish. Cover the bottom of the dish with about $^1/_3$ of the bread slices, butter-and-marmalade sides up (you may have to cut a few slices in half to make a good fit). Place a single layer of half the apple slices on top. Scatter half of the cranberries or raisins over the apples. Repeat with another layer of bread, the remaining apples, and the remaining cranberries or raisins. Finish with a layer of bread, butter-and-marmalade sides down.

3   In a bowl, whisk the eggs, vanilla, and Grand Marnier or Cointreau together. Add the milk and cream and whisk to thoroughly combine. Pour over the bread. Use your hands to press down the bread to assure that the top layer has been saturated with the liquid. Evenly distribute the sugar over the top. Bake for 45 minutes, or until the custard is set and the top layer is golden. Place under a preheated broiler for exactly 2 minutes to caramelize the top. Let cool on a wire rack for at least 30 minutes before serving. Serve warm or at room temperature.

SERVES 8

PUMPKIN CARAMEL
PUDDING

Martha Fish made this entry in her diary on November 27, 1884:
"Thanksgiving Day, had puddings as usual...." I suggest that you follow Martha's
Thanksgiving tradition and serve this pumpkin pudding instead of
pumpkin pie for a change.

3/4 cup plus 2/3 cup sugar

1/3 cup water

6 large eggs

2 cups pumpkin purée

1/2 teaspoon salt

1/2 rounded teaspoon ground
    ginger

1/2 rounded teaspoon ground
    cinnamon

1/4 rounded teaspoon ground cloves

3 cups heavy cream

Thinly julienned crystallized ginger
    for garnish

1   In a small saucepan, combine the 3/4 cup sugar with the water. Bring to a boil, stirring with a wooden spoon and washing down the sides of the pan once or twice with a wet pastry brush. Cook the syrup until it's amber-colored. Immediately remove from heat and pour into an 8-cup charlotte mold or loaf pan. Repeatedly tilt the mold in a circular motion until the sides and bottom are evenly coated. Set aside and let harden.

2   Preheat an oven to 350°F. In a large bowl, using a whisk, beat the eggs with the 2/3 cup sugar. Add the pumpkin, salt, ginger, cinnamon, cloves, and 2 cups of the heavy cream and whisk until smooth. Pour the mixture into the caramel-lined mold. Place the mold in a baking pan and fill the baking pan with hot water. If using a charlotte mold, the water will only reach one fourth to one third of the way up the sides of the mold. If using a loaf pan, let the water reach halfway up the sides. Bake for 1 hour and 15 minutes to 2 hours (the loaf will cook faster than the mold), or until a tester inserted in the center comes out clean. Let the pudding cool, then refrigerate it for at least 4 hours or, preferably, overnight.

3   Just before serving, whip the remaining 1 cup cream until stiff. Fill a pastry bag fitted with a wide fluted tip with the cream.

4   To serve, run a knife around the edge of the mold and invert the mold onto a platter. Decorate the pudding and the platter with rosettes of whipped cream. Decorate the rosettes with the julienned ginger.

SERVES 8 TO 10

INDIAN PUDDING WITH HARD SAUCE

My friend Steve Bender, who generously gave me recipes for this book and for The Nantucket Table, *ran one of Nantucket's best tables when he owned the delightful and sorely missed Sandpiper Restaurant on Main Street. In its heyday, the Sandpiper was the place for an early morning breakfast before heading out to the beach, and for a late-night bite after a few drinks at the Bosun's Locker, just across the street. But it was the Sandpiper's 99¢ (!) special that has remained with me forever: a bowl of chowder with a roll and butter (and crackers), a beverage, and a parfait glass filled with Indian pudding, topped with a scoop of vanilla ice cream. It doesn't get any better than that. ¶With deference to Steve, here's my version of a truly American dish. If you like, use vanilla ice cream or whipped cream as a topping in place of the hard sauce.*

FOR THE HARD SAUCE
$1/2$ cup unsalted butter at room temperature
I cup confectioners' sugar
I tablespoon dark rum

FOR THE INDIAN PUDDING
5 cups whole milk
$1/2$ cup cornmeal
I teaspoon salt
2 tablespoons unsalted butter
$1/4$ cup molasses
$1/2$ cup maple syrup
2 large eggs, lightly beaten
$1/3$ cup dried cranberries or raisins

1   Make the hard sauce: In a bowl, blend the softened $1/2$ cup butter, confectioners' sugar, and rum until smooth. Transfer to a smaller bowl or storage container and refrigerate.

2   Make the pudding: In a large nonreactive saucepan over medium heat, scald the milk. Reduce heat to a simmer, and slowly add the cornmeal while stirring constantly. Cook, stirring occasionally, for 25 minutes, or until the mixture is thickened to the consistency of yogurt (you may want to do this in a double boiler, because if you're not careful, the milk and cornmeal will make an enamel-like coating on the bottom of your pan). Stir in the salt, butter, molasses, maple syrup, eggs, and cranberries or raisins until thoroughly combined. Remove from heat.

3   Preheat an oven to 300°F. Butter a 6- or 8-cup baking dish. Pour the cornmeal mixture into the prepared dish. Bake for 2 hours, or until the pudding is set and a tester inserted in the center of the pudding comes away clean. It won't be firm. Place on a wire rack and let cool just enough to allow excess liquid to be absorbed, about 1 hour. Serve warm, each serving topped with a rounded tablespoon of hard sauce.

The pudding can be made ahead and reheated to serve.

SERVES 8

NATIVE AMERICANS, CORN, *and* NANTUCKET

Indian pudding is not a Native American dessert. Indian pudding, or hasty pudding, as it's sometimes called, is the simple American version of a classic English steamed pudding, using cornmeal instead of wheat flour. The Native Americans introduced corn to the colonists. The ingenious natives, who methodically planted fields of corn in neat rows of mounds, each one containing a kernel and a fish, taught this way of gardening to their neighbors.

With the same ingenuity, according to Native American legend, a giant god named Maushop created Nantucket. Maushop, a resident of Martha's Vineyard, would often invite the Indians to dine with him. Once, to show their gratitude, they gave him a gift of tobacco. Maushop filled his pipe with the gift, smoked it, then dumped the ashes into the sea, which became the Island of Nantucket.

GIFTS OF
FOOD

A QUARTET OF MARMALADES

Marmalade making is sometimes a daunting process and mistakes are easily made. My friend Helen Potter, who lives in Australia, concludes her explicit ten-page letter of marmalade-making tips by saying, "If you meet an Englishwoman, pick her brains! Take her home! Propose a [marmalade] cooking bee," alluding of course to the British obsession with marmalade. ¶Forewarned and filled with trepidation, I set out to make marmalade. Further research helped me develop a useful marmalade mantra: It's a suspension (key word) of fruit and peel in jelly. Remove the pith, cut the zest very thinly, cook the fruit, not the sugar—and they came out beautifully. ¶Marmalades, most always but not exclusively made with citrus fruits, are the ideal winter holiday gift, a bit of sunshine when it's most needed.

SWEET NAVEL-ORANGE MARMALADE

6 large navel oranges
2 large lemons
6 cups water
3 cups sugar

1   Scrub the oranges and lemons with a stiff brush under cold running water. Use a very sharp paring knife or a good vegetable peeler to remove the zest from the fruit, leaving the bitter white pith. Finely dice the zest. Put the diced zest in a large nonreactive bowl. Using a sharp paring knife, carefully cut the pith from the fruit. Use the knife to cut the fruit sections from between the membranes. Add the orange and lemon sections to the bowl and use your hands to squeeze the juice from the membranes into the bowl. Add the water. Cover with plastic wrap and let sit overnight.

2   Place the contents of the bowl in a large nonreactive stockpot or a copper jam pot over high heat. Bring to a boil. Reduce heat and simmer for 1 hour. Add the sugar. Bring to a boil, reduce heat, and simmer until a candy thermometer reaches 220°F, 30 to 40 minutes. Remove from heat and let rest for 30 minutes.

3   Pour the mixture into hot sterilized half-pint jars, seal, and process in a boiling-water bath according to the manufacturer's directions.

NOTE   I like to let the marmalade settle for a week or so before using it.

MAKES ABOUT 4 PINTS

PINK GRAPEFRUIT MARMALADE

3 large, heavy pink grapefruits
   (about 4 pounds total)
2 lemons
5 cups water
4 cups sugar

1   Scrub the grapefruits and lemons with a stiff brush under cold running water. Using a very sharp paring knife or good vegetable peeler, remove the zest from the fruit in 1-inch strips, leaving the bitter white pith. Cut the zest on the diagonal into thin julienne. Put the julienne in a large nonreactive bowl. Use a sharp paring knife to carefully cut the pith from the fruit. Then use the same knife to cut the fruit sections from between the membranes. Add the sections to the bowl and use your hands to squeeze the juice from the membranes into the bowl. Add the water, cover with plastic wrap, and let sit overnight.

2   Empty the bowl into a large nonreactive stockpot or a copper jam pot over high heat. Bring to a boil. Reduce heat and simmer for 1 hour. Stir in the sugar. Bring to a boil, reduce heat, and simmer until a candy thermometer registers 220°F, 30 to 45 minutes. Remove from heat and let stand for 30 minutes.

3   Pour the mixture into hot sterilized half-pint jars, seal, and process in a boiling-water bath according to the manufacturer's directions.

MAKES ABOUT 4 PINTS

TANGERINE MARMALADE

6 large tangerines
2 lemons
6 cups water
3 cups sugar

1   Using a stiff brush, scrub the tangerines and lemons under cold running water. Using a sharp paring knife or good vegetable peeler, remove the zest from the fruit, leaving the bitter white pith. Cut the zest on the diagonal into thin julienne. Put the julienne in a large nonreactive bowl. Using a sharp knife, carefully cut the pith from the fruit. Using the same knife, remove the fruit sections from between the membranes. Add the tangerine and lemon sections to the bowl. Use your hands to squeeze the juice from the membranes into the bowl. Add the water. Cover with plastic wrap and let sit overnight.

2   Empty the bowl into a large nonreactive stockpot or a copper jam pot over high heat. Bring to a boil. Reduce heat and simmer for 1 hour. Stir in the sugar. Bring to a boil, reduce heat, and simmer until a candy thermometer registers 220°F, 30 to 45 minutes. Remove from heat and let stand for 30 minutes.

3   Pour the mixture into hot sterilized half-pint jars, seal, and process in a boiling-water bath according to the manufacturer's directions.

MAKES ABOUT 4 PINTS

LEMON-LIME MARMALADE

4 large lemons
4 large limes
6 cups water
5 cups sugar

1   Using a stiff brush, scrub the lemons and limes under cold running water. Use a very sharp paring knife or a slicing knife to cut the fruit into the thinnest possible slices. Remove the seeds. Cut the slices into quarters. Put the fruit in a large nonreactive bowl. Add the water. Cover with plastic wrap and let sit overnight.

2   Empty the bowl into a large nonreactive stockpot or a copper jam pot over high heat. Bring to a boil. Reduce heat and simmer for 1 hour. Stir in the sugar. Bring to a boil, reduce heat, and simmer until a candy thermometer registers 220°F, 30 to 45 minutes. Remove from heat and let stand for 30 minutes.

3   Pour the mixture into hot sterilized half-pint jars, seal, and process in a boiling-water bath according to the manufacturer's directions.

MAKES ABOUT 4 PINTS

GREEN TOMATO PRESERVES

The first frost arrives in Nantucket a bit later than it does on the mainland, so there's more time to think about preparations for all those green tomatoes that are sure to be left hanging on the vines. This recipe was given to me by my friend Rose, and it's the tastiest recipe for green tomatoes, including fried ones, that I've ever had. ¶When you make your labels, add some serving suggestions, such as "Great with roast meats, especially ham; delicious on buttery English muffins; and exceptional with a toasted spicy cheese sandwich." This gift will have such success that next year you won't wait for the frost to pick green tomatoes.

5 pounds green tomatoes, washed
   and coarsely chopped
5 pounds sugar
6 limes, scrubbed and cut into
   eighths
1 teaspoon salt

1   In a very large nonreactive stockpot or copper jam pot over medium heat, combine the tomatoes, sugar, limes, and salt. Bring to a simmer and cook, stirring occasionally, until a candy thermometer registers 220°F, about 1 hour. Be careful not to overcook, or the sugar will begin to caramelize and will harden when cool.

2   Pour the mixture into hot sterilized half-pint jars, seal, and process in a boiling-water bath according to the manufacturer's directions. Store in a cool dark place.

MAKES 8 TO 10 HALF-PINTS

CRANBERRY CONSERVE

*Reva Schlesinger, whose historically correct home was used for the
Chanukah photographs in this book, shared this recipe for cranberry conserve with
me. It's her adaptation of a recipe from the very informative* The Martha's Vineyard
Cookbook *(Harper & Row, 1971). Reva and I mused for a minute,
fully aware of the friendly rivalry between the two islands, about a Vineyard
recipe destined for a Nantucket book. Reva solved the question easily:
"They've got the recipe, but we've got the cranberries!" This is one gift that
the receiver is sure to enjoy.*

8 cups cranberries, picked over
 and rinsed

3 cups water

3 1/2 cups sugar

2 oranges, cut in pieces, then
 coarsely chopped in a food
 processor (reserve juice)

2 lemons, cut in pieces, then
 coarsely chopped in a food
 processor (reserve juice)

5 tablespoons coarsely chopped
 crystallized ginger

2 cups pecans, coarsely chopped

1/2 cup Grand Marnier or other
 orange liqueur

1   In a large (at least 8 quarts), heavy-bottomed nonreactive stockpot over medium-high heat, cook the cranberries in the water until
they pop.

2   Stir in the sugar, chopped oranges and juice, chopped lemons and
juice, and chopped ginger. Bring to a boil. Reduce heat to medium
and simmer, stirring frequently, until the mixture is thick and
clear. Place a small amount of the syrup on a spoon and raise it
from the pot; if large drops form on each side, the conserve is ready
to remove from heat.

3   Stir in the pecans and Grand Marnier.

4   Pour the mixture into hot sterilized half-pint jars, seal, and
process in a boiling-water bath according to the manufacturer's
directions.

MAKES 6 PINTS

CRANBERRY SYRUP

Here's one more recipe for the ubiquitous cranberry. Try this syrup mixed with sparkling water, swirled through plain yogurt or vanilla ice cream, as a topping for pancakes, or combined with vodka and tonic in a drink I call "'Twas the Night Before Christmas" (recipe follows). ¶Search out pretty bottles or jars when giving the syrup for gifts. Attach a label and suggestions for use.

4 cups sugar

6 cups water

6 cups cranberries, picked over, rinsed, and coarsely ground in a food processor

1   In a large nonreactive saucepan, combine the sugar and water. Bring to a boil and cook for 5 minutes. Add the berries, reduce heat, and simmer for 15 minutes. Remove from heat.

2   Place a sieve over a bowl. Line the sieve with cheesecloth. Add the cranberries to the sieve in batches. Press the berries with the back of a large spoon until every possible drop of syrup goes through the sieve.

3   Pour the mixture into hot sterilized jars, seal, and process in a boiling-water bath according to the manufacturer's directions. Keep some for yourself and try the drink recipe below. The syrup will keep for up to 6 months in an airtight container.

MAKES 6 TO 8 CUPS

'TWAS THE NIGHT BEFORE CHRISTMAS

Fill an 8-ounce glass with ice. Add the cranberry syrup and vodka and stir. Fill the glass with tonic water and add the lime slice to the glass. Stir and serve.

MAKES 1 DRINK

3 tablespoons cranberry syrup, above

2 tablespoons vodka

Tonic water

1 slice lime

HOLIDAY PARTY MIX

*William Holland, Nantucket purveyor of groceries, whose December 14, 1912,
ad in* The Inquirer and Mirror *I've already cited in another recipe, included
a bold banner touting "fruits, nuts, candies, etc." I can speculate that a creative
Nantucketer may have put together a mix like this one,
with Mr. Holland's wares, to brighten a holiday party.*

4 cups salted shelled pistachios
4 cups salted cashews
4 cups honey-roasted peanuts
2 cups dried cranberries
2 cups thinly julienned dried
    apricots
1 cup thinly julienned crystallized
    ginger

1 Toss together the nuts, fruits, and ginger in a large bowl. Store
in airtight containers in a cool, dry spot until ready for use.
Package in clear cellophane bags. Close and tie with a bow using
a pretty cloth ribbon. Label.

MAKES SIX 1-POUND BAGS

CURRY BOWS

Energetic Chin Manasmontri, native of Bangkok and citizen of Nantucket, taught me the most unusual things that I know how to cook. Fast-talking and fast-moving, Chin, ex-caterer, ex-restaurateur (of the Island's first Thai-Chinese restaurant), and lightship basket maker, has revealed the wonders of his country's cooking to me over the past decades. I'm eternally grateful to Chin for his willingness to share his recipe for curry bows. An exotic chip, they are the perfect cocktail snack. Packed in cellophane bags and secured with a green and red plaid ribbon, they are the holiday present that will receive more thanks and compliments than any other gift you give. I promise.

1 pound eggroll skins (found in the frozen food department of most supermarkets)

1 rounded tablespoon salt

3 tablespoons good-quality curry powder

4 cups corn or another vegetable oil

1   Place the stack of eggroll skins on a cutting board. Cut it into 8 equal strips. Beginning with the top layer, pick up 1 strip at a time and tie a loose knot. Store the tied knots on a baking sheet (they can be piled on top of each other). Continue to tie the skins into knots a layer at a time, rather than a stack at a time.

2   Put the salt and curry powder in a bowl and stir to combine. Put the mixture in a large salt or sugar shaker. In a large skillet, heat the oil to 350°F.

3   Add the bows to the hot oil a handful at a time. They will puff up and sizzle as soon as they hit the oil. Use a wooden chopstick to quickly flip them over and separate any that may have stuck together, and cook until the bows are pale gold. Move very, very quickly; this operation should take seconds, as the bows can over-cook in a blink of an eye. Using a wire-mesh strainer, transfer the bows to paper towels to drain and cool. Immediately add another handful to the oil. While they're cooking, shake the curry-salt mix-ture on the cooling bows. You have to be slightly ambidextrous for this procedure: If you stop to shake the curry-salt on the bows and leave the skillet empty, the oil will overheat and burn the next batch of bows.

4   Make labels. Apply them to cellophane bags, not plastic ones. Pack the cooled curry bows into the labeled bags. Secure the bags with a ribbon bow. The curry bows will keep for up to 2 weeks stored in a cool, dry place.

the SHOPPER'S STROLL

In 1974, the Nantucket Chamber of Commerce created the Shopper's Stroll to encourage Nantucketers to stay on the Island to do their holiday shopping. The idea was for local shopkeepers to keep their businesses open late on a Friday evening in mid-December when the Main Street Christmas trees were lighted. With a flip of a switch, Main Street sparkled, shop doors were flung open, and shoppers were enticed inside by the spicy fragrances of hot mulled wine, spiked cider, eggnog, and all sorts of baked goods to snack on. Santa Claus rode down to Main Street in a horse-drawn carriage and stopped at the fountain at the foot of the street to listen to the wishes of any child brave enough to sit on his lap.

The air of small-town bonhomie was soon interrupted when word of the Island's charming event spread to the far reaches of the Mainland. The press picked up on it, and soon the Friday-evening affair became an activity-packed weekend; Santa now arrives on a Coast Guard cutter.

Today, Shopper's Stroll has become the largest single retail day (Saturday) of the year on Nantucket.

CARAMELIZED DRIED FRUITS AND NUTS

Hannah Maria Allen, aboard the bark Sea Ranger *with her husband, Captain Charles E. Allen, mailed a letter (via San Francisco) dated January 1, 1871, to her daughters Emma and Lillian, back in Nantucket. "How did you enjoy Christmas? Rollie [son Rollin, traveling with his parents] hung up his Christmas stocking but all the poor little fellow got was a few raisins. A ship is a poor place for Christmas presents...." ¶Dried fruits and nuts are traditional Christmas gifts, whether baked into a fruitcake, covered with chocolate, or tucked in a salty stocking. A cigar box lined with a pretty paper doily is the ideal way to pack these caramelized fruit-and-nut-loaded skewers.*

6 dried figs, halved
6 dried apricots, halved
12 dried, pitted dates
24 shelled pecans or walnuts,
    or a combination of both
1/3 cup water
1 1/2 cups sugar

1   Thread 5 assorted fruit pieces and nuts on each of twelve 6-inch bamboo skewers. If not carefully eased onto the skewer, the nuts are likely to split. I solve this problem by positioning the nuts between the sticky, cut sides of the figs and the apricots, "gluing" them onto the skewers.

2   In a small saucepan over medium heat, combine the water and the sugar. Bring to a boil, stirring and scraping with a wooden spoon and brushing the sides of the pan once or twice with a wet pastry brush. Cook the syrup until it's pale amber-colored. Remove from heat, tilt the pan to the side, and quickly swirl each fruit-and-nut-loaded skewer in the caramel. Immediately place the skewers on waxed or parchment paper to harden. Store in a cool, dry spot until ready to use. If properly stored in an airtight container these skewers will keep for up to 3 months.

MAKES TWELVE 6-INCH SKEWERS OF FRUITS AND NUTS

HILDA SIMON'S GINGERSNAPS

My late mother, Hilda, always served these cookies to her customers at her Main Street shop, The Calico Whale, on Nantucket's Shopper's Stroll weekend. ¶When I opened my catering/take-out food shop in New York City, I offered these gingersnaps for sale. Throughout the year, I sold the one-inch cookies by the pound from a big glass jar on the counter, but during the winter holiday season, I filled clear cellophane bags with cookies and tied each bag with red and green ribbons. Those pretty bags flew off the counter faster than I could replace them! ¶Please your friends with a gift bag or special tin (see Note) of Hilda's gingersnaps. They are easier to make and package (and much more satisfying) than ordering a gift from a catalogue.

1½ cups vegetable shortening
2 cups sugar, plus extra for
    sprinkling
2 eggs
4 cups all-purpose flour
2 teaspoons baking soda
2 teaspoons ground cinnamon
2 teaspoons ground cloves
2 teaspoons ground ginger
½ cup dark molasses

1   Preheat an oven to 350°F. In a large bowl, cream the shortening and sugar together until light and fluffy. Beat in the eggs well.

2   Sift the flour, baking soda, and spices together. Add the molasses and dry ingredients to the shortening mixture. Beat to combine.

3   Shape the dough into 1-inch balls and place 2 inches apart on greased baking sheets. Sprinkle with sugar.

4   Bake for 12 to 15 minutes, or until the outside edge begins to crisp and turn slightly darker and the middle is still soft. Transfer to a wire rack to cool.

NOTE   To order wonderful trompe l'oeil Nantucket lightship basket tins, call Weeds at (508) 228-5202.

MAKES ABOUT 5 DOZEN COOKIES

DATE PUDDING

My friend Rose Inghram shared this recipe with me that has been in her family for at least 150 years. She told me that the pudding was her childhood Christmas dessert, invariably served with bourbon-flavored whipped cream. However, as long as I've known Rose, she's given this pudding, cut into little squares and colorfully bundled, as a "bonus" gift during the winter holidays. Much more interesting and, to my palate, tastier than traditional fruitcake, this date pudding is also easier to make. ¶The white cardboard take-out containers used by Chinese restaurants are the ideal packages for these date-and-nut squares. Line the containers with a square of brightly colored cellophane and decorate the outside with holiday good wishes scribbled with gold and silver markers.

$1^{1}/_{2}$ cups coarsely chopped dates
I cup coarsely chopped walnuts
3 rounded tablespoons flour
$^{1}/_{2}$ cup sugar
I teaspoon baking powder
I tablespoon unsalted butter, melted
2 eggs, lightly beaten

1   In a medium bowl, combine the dates, nuts, flour, sugar, baking powder, melted butter, and eggs and stir until thoroughly blended.

2   Generously butter an 8-inch square baking pan. Pour the batter into the pan. Use a rubber spatula to evenly distribute the batter. Bake for 30 minutes, or until a tester inserted in the center comes out clean. Let cool on a wire rack. Cut into sixteen 2-inch squares. Store in an airtight container for up to 2 weeks. These freeze perfectly.

MAKES SIXTEEN 2-INCH SQUARES

MARSHMALLOWS
AND HOT COCOA MIX

Jackie Boisse, chef-around-Nantucket, was a guest at the same holiday dinner party as I was a few years ago and brought a knock-out hostess gift: homemade marshmallows and a jarful of hot cocoa mix. ¶With Jackie's gracious permission, I've borrowed her idea for this book. A boxful of homemade marshmallows, a tin of cocoa mix, and a couple of colorful mugs—can you imagine a better present?

FOR THE MARSHMALLOWS

3 packages unflavored gelatin

I cup water

1 1/2 teaspoons pure vanilla extract

1/8 teaspoon salt

I cup light corn syrup

2 1/4 cups granulated sugar

I cup confectioners' sugar for
      coating

FOR THE COCOA MIX

2 cups dry milk

2/3 cup good-quality Dutch-process
      powdered cocoa

2/3 cup granulated sugar

2 teaspoons ground cinnamon

1   Make the marshmallows: Line a 9-inch square baking dish or an 8-by-12-inch baking dish with waxed paper and coat with vegetable-oil cooking spray.

2   In the bowl of an electric mixer, combine the gelatin, 1/2 cup of the water, the vanilla, and salt. Set aside.

3   In a medium saucepan, combine the remaining 1/2 cup water, the corn syrup, and the 2 1/4 cups sugar. Bring to a boil and cook to the soft-ball stage, 240°F on a candy thermometer.

4   Pour the hot mixture into the gelatin mixture. Beat with an electric mixer until it is so thick that the beaters stop moving, 7 to 10 minutes. The mixture should be pure white and shiny. Pour the mixture into the prepared baking dish. Tilt back and forth to evenly distribute. Let sit uncovered, at room temperature, overnight.

5   Cover a cutting board with a thin film of confectioners' sugar. Unmold the marshmallow mixture onto the cutting board. Cut into squares, or use simple shaped cookie cutters to make hearts, Christmas trees, stars, etc. Coat all sides of the cut marshmallows with confectioners' sugar. Use now, or store in an airtight container in a cool, dry spot for up to 2 months.

6   Make the cocoa mix: Combine all the ingredients in a large bowl. Package the mix in pretty jars or tins and make labels that include these directions: Put 2 rounded tablespoons of the cocoa mix into an 8-ounce mug. Add boiling water and stir to dissolve the powder. Serve with 1 or 2 marshmallows.

NOTE   The cocoa mix is purposely not too sweet, to accommodate the very sweet marshmallows.

MAKES 8 TO 24 MARSHMALLOWS AND 32 OUNCES HOT COCOA MIX

LEILA COFFIN RAY'S
POTATO FUDGE

Leila Coffin Ray taught home economics at the Coffin School during the first half of the twentieth century. This potato fudge recipe, given to me by her daughter, Jane Richmond, class of 1947, was a much requested lesson from Mrs. Ray's students. ¶The recipe came with a couple of caveats: 1. Don't double the recipe. 2. Don't make it on a hot or humid day, or it won't set. ¶I suggest that you put the fudge squares in paper mini-muffin cups for packaging.

One 3- to 4-ounce unpeeled potato
1 pound confectioners' sugar
1½ cups firmly packed shredded
    coconut
2 rounded teaspoons cornstarch
3 ounces unsweetened chocolate,
    chopped
1 teaspoon pure vanilla extract

1   Cook the potato in boiling water to cover until a tester easily passes through it. Peel it while still hot and thoroughly mash in a large bowl. Add the confectioners' sugar and stir until the mixture is stiff and smooth. Add the coconut and blend in.

2   Dust an 8-inch square baking pan with the cornstarch. Add the potato mixture and evenly spread to cover the bottom. Let sit for 30 minutes.

3   In a small saucepan over barely simmering water, melt the chocolate with the vanilla. Evenly spread the chocolate over the potato mixture. Score the squares and let the chocolate set. Cut into squares and use now, or store in an airtight container in a cool, dry spot for up to 2 weeks.

MAKES 16 SQUARES

the COFFIN SCHOOL

To honor his Nantucket ancestry (he was a descendant of original English settler Tristam Coffin), Admiral Sir Isaac Coffin, a veteran of the Royal Navy, created a public school on the Island. Through the years, the school changed not only its location, from Fair Street to its present location on Winter Street, but also its doctrine. It began as student-monitored classrooms where a traditional education was offered, and became a school envisioned by another Coffin, Elizabeth Rebecca, where manual skills and home economics were taught. Those skills became the backbone of a new Nantucket economy, replacing the one that had been recently devastated by the end of the whaling era. Now, young men and women would have the knowledge and means to find trades to service the year-round residents and the burgeoning summertime population. Boys learned woodworking, metalwork, plumbing, and electricity, and girls learned to sew, cook, and make baskets.

Although the Coffin School no longer functions as a primary public school, under the aegis of the Egan Institute for Maritime Studies it continues to offer interesting programs and classes in a great variety of subjects. Additionally, it's a beautifully restored Greek Revival building that's open to the public.

Sir Isaac would be pleased and satisfied that his academy still brings honor to his name.

ACKNOWLEDGMENTS A good book is the result of the collaboration and coöperation of many generous people. This book is no exception.

I begin my thanks and gratitude with Marian Young, my agent, who's always there.

Bill LeBlond at Chronicle Books, a fellow New Englander, far away on the other coast, there (here), in spirit. The staff at Chronicle: Stephanie Rosenbaum, Michele Fuller, Pamela Geismar, Steve Moore, and Carolyn Miller, all patient and helpful. And to Anne Galperin whose design for the book perfectly conjures a Nantucket holiday.

Nantucket-based photographer Jeffrey Allen, who got up at three in the morning on Christmas Eve day to capture the first snowfall of the year for this book, you're a hero! Jeff's silent, skilled assistant, Bob Frazier, was a graceful presence on the shoots. My assistant, Ron Elder, organized and good-natured, made everything easy.

On Nantucket, as usual, a community of friends, old and new, opened their homes and hearts, and lent memories, props, and information: Dan and Nancy Bills of The Lion's Paw, George Davis of Weeds, Kathy Hay, Christine and Edward Sanford, Pam Myers, Reva and Mort Schlesinger, Reggie Levine, Karen Pelrine and Douglas Pinney, Samantha Rand, Steve and Anna Bender, Jane Richmond, Jackie Boisse, Janet Folger, Nat Philbrick, Mimi Beman, Elin Anderwald, Christie Cure, Peter Kaizer, Gwen Gaillard, Zelda Zlotin, Irean and Herbert Schreiber, Michael and Rona Galvin, Dede Avery, Thom Koon, and at the Nantucket Historical Association big thanks to generous, resourceful Libby Oldham, and Betsy Lowenstein.

On the mainland, I'm grateful for the help, advice, and encouragement of old friends Rose Inghram, Helen Potter, Nally Bellati, John Derian, and Roy Finamore (who also contributed a couple of scrumptious recipes).

Peggy Eastman, on Cape Cod, gave me good information about the Quakers.

Susan Kirby worked magic on the computer.

My real family on Nantucket, Laura Simon and Jimmy Gross, as always gave me the safety net of their home, truck, vegetables, eggs, and honey, as well as their sympathetic and knowledgeable ears whenever needed.

And, of course, Musetta, the dog with the most frequent-flier miles, I'm so glad you're still here.

Huge thanks to everyone, and happy holidays, now, and forever.

SOURCES   The following excerpts and quotes appear courtesy of the Edouard A. Stackpole Research Center and Library, Nantucket Historical Association, Nantucket, Massachusetts:

p. 44   Martha Fish Papers/Louise Henry Collection (MS 380)

p. 51   Edouard A. Stackpole Collection (MS 335)

p. 59   William B. Starbuck Journals, 1873–1890 (MS 363)

p. 63   William B. Starbuck Journals, 1873–1890 (MS 363)

p. 71   Sharp Family Papers (MS 270)

p. 72   Sharp Family Papers (MS 270)

p. 106   "Old-Time Thanksgiving Dinner at Nantucket," by Lilian Clisby Bridgham, 19th century, Edouard A. Stackpole Collection (MS 335)

p. 110   Marshall-Pinkham Family Papers/Brown Collection, 1850–1872 (MS 283)

p. 123   Charles Neal Barney Collection (MS 304)

p. 136   Martha Fish Papers/Louise Henry Collection (MS 380)

p. 152   Allen Family Papers/Marjorie Tyrie Collection (MS 308)

INDEX

A

TABLE *of* EQUIVALENTS

LIQUID/DRY MEASURES

U.S.	METRIC
$1/4$ teaspoon	1.25 milliliters
$1/2$ teaspoon	2.5 milliliters
1 teaspoon	5 milliliters
1 tablespoon (3 teaspoons)	15 milliliters
1 fluid ounce (2 tablespoons)	30 milliliters
$1/4$ cup	60 milliliters
$1/3$ cup	80 milliliters
$1/2$ cup	120 milliliters
1 cup	240 milliliters
1 pint (2 cups)	480 milliliters
1 quart (4 cups, 32 ounces)	960 milliliters
1 gallon (4 quarts)	3.84 liters
1 ounce (by weight)	28 grams
1 pound	454 grams
2.2 pounds	1 kilogram

LENGTH

U.S.	METRIC
$1/8$ inch	3 millimeters
$1/4$ inch	6 millimeters
$1/2$ inch	12 millimeters
1 inch	2.5 centimeters

OVEN TEMPERATURES

FAHRENHEIT	CELSIUS	GAS
250	120	$1/2$
275	140	1
300	150	2
325	160	3
350	180	4
375	190	5
400	200	6
425	220	7
450	230	8
475	240	9
500	260	10